AI for Everyday Automation

7 AI workflows to save hours at work every week

Dipankar Sarkar

<packt>

AI for Everyday Automation

Portfolio Director: Pavan Ramchandani
Relationship Lead: Larissa Pinto
Program Manager: Divij Kotian
Content Engineer: Akanksha Gupta
Technical Editor: Vidhisha Patidar
Indexer: Rekha Nair
Production Designer: Alishon Falcon
Growth Lead: Nivedita Singh

First published: June 2026

Production reference: 1240626

Published by Packt Publishing Ltd.
Grosvenor House
11 St Paul's Square
Birmingham
B3 1RB, UK.

ISBN 978-1-80808-981-7
`www.packtpub.com`

For Maitrayee, whose constant support makes everything possible.

For our two sons, who make every day an adventure.

And in memory of my father, Amal, who taught me that the best work is done with patience and precision.

– Dipankar Sarkar

Contributors

About the author

Dipankar Sarkar is a Principal Engineer at Neul Labs where he builds open-source agentic AI tools. He previously served as Principal AI Architect at Aveni, an FCA-regulated fintech, where he worked at the intersection of AI capability and real-world deployment. He has filed multiple patents in generative AI and communication technologies.

Dipankar holds a BTech in Computer Science and Engineering from IIT Delhi and an MS in Cybersecurity from Arizona State University. He is a published author and a machine learning researcher. He lives in Scotland with his wife and two sons.

This book exists because of the people who made it possible.

To my wife, Maitrayee, your constant support is the foundation everything else stands on. Your patience during long writing sessions, your sharp eye on early drafts, and your steady belief that this book would be worth the effort carried me through. Thank you for being my first reader and my most honest critic.

To our two sons, you are too young to read this, but old enough to have noticed that Dada was on his laptop more than usual. Thank you for the interruptions. They were the best parts of my day.

To my mother, for the discipline that makes a book possible, and the curiosity that makes it interesting. To my sister, for your constant encouragement and for always asking how the writing was going, even when the answer was, "slowly."

To my father, Amal, I wish you were here to hold this book. The scientific rigor you brought to your own work taught me how to bring the same to mine. This one is for you.

To my father-in-law and mother-in-law, for your warmth, your generosity, and the space you gave me to think and write. I am grateful.

To the team at Packt, thank you for believing that a concise book about AI workflows could be as valuable as a 500-page textbook, and for pushing it to be sharper and more practical at every turn.

To my colleagues at Neul Labs and Skelf Research, the ideas in this book were tested in our daily work before they were written down. Thank you for being the proving ground.

And to every professional who picked up this book hoping to reclaim their time: I wrote it for you.

About the reviewer

Thomas Rice is a business automation leader, solution architect, and delivery strategist with over 20 years of experience turning complex challenges into scalable, practical solutions. He specializes in Microsoft technologies—especially the Power Platform—to simplify processes, accelerate delivery, and drive measurable outcomes.

A Microsoft Community Super User, he guides teams on architecture, governance, and best practices to build secure, sustainable solutions. He is passionate about continuous learning, mentoring others, and delivering real business value.

Table of Contents

Preface

This book starts with a simple premise: You are good at your job; you just spend too much time with administrative redundancies. Buried under emails, meetings, status reports, task tracking, research rabbit holes, and the endless cycle of reformatting information, the actual thinking—strategy, decision-making, and creative work—becomes an afterthought.

This book is about eliminating the scaffolding.

AI tools like Claude, ChatGPT, and Perplexity are not productivity toys or clever search engines. When connected to the tools you already use, your email, calendar, documents, and task tracker, they become infrastructure for your workday. They read your inbox and draft replies in your voice. They process meeting transcripts and push action items directly to your project tracker. They search the web and your internal documents simultaneously to produce sourced research briefs. They turn a week of meeting notes into a status report, save it to your Drive, and email it to your manager. All from a single conversation.

This is not simply a book of AI prompts but also a book of connected workflows that you install as Skills in your AI tool, run by talking naturally, and refine over time. Every workflow was built and tested in real professional environments, from regulated fintech to open-source AI infrastructure to academic research, before being written down.

By the end of your first week with this book, the goal is to reclaim 8 to 12 hours. This won't happen by working faster, but by eliminating the work that was never yours to do in the first place.

Who this book is for

This book is for mid-career knowledge workers: product managers, consultants, team leads, analysts, operations managers, and small-team founders who spend 60% or more of their day on communication, reporting, research, and coordination rather than deep creative or strategic work. You have tried AI tools casually but have not built repeatable daily workflows. You want immediate, practical results, not theory.

You do not need to be technical. If you can use a web browser, install an app, and upload a file, you have all the skills required. This book never asks you to write code, use a terminal, or understand how AI models work.

What this book covers

Chapter 1: Audit, Arm, Go, helps you identify which tasks eat your time, set up your AI tools with your personal context, and build your automation hit list.

Chapter 2, Your First AI Win, walks you through completing your first real AI-assisted task in under 30 minutes, establishing the core loop you will use throughout the book.

Chapter 3, Inbox Zero in 25 Minutes, connects your Gmail to your AI tool so it reads, classifies, drafts, and sends email, introducing the connected workflow pattern that powers every subsequent chapter.

Chapter 4, Meetings That Actually Work, automates the entire meeting lifecycle: AI reads your calendar for briefs, processes transcripts into structured packets, creates tasks in your tracker, and sends summaries via email.

Chapter 5, Research in 30 Minutes, Not 3 Hours, uses AI that searches the web and reads your internal documents to produce sourced, structured research briefs with confidence levels.

Chapter 6, First Drafts in 15 Minutes, builds document generation chains where AI gathers inputs from Drive, email, and task tools, drafts the document, and delivers it, all in one conversation.

Chapter 7, Tracked Tasks in 15 Minutes, extracts action items from meetings, emails, and documents and pushes them directly to your project tracker so nothing falls through the cracks.

Chapter 8, Spreadsheets Without Writing Formulas, cleans, analyzes, charts, and summarizes data by describing what you want in plain English, with AI running the code behind the scenes.

Chapter 9, Write Once, Use Everywhere, turns a single set of source material into LinkedIn posts, internal announcements, client emails, presentation bullets, and newsletter sections, distributed from one conversation.

Chapter 10, Your Automated Week, assembles all workflows into a weekly system, walks you through installing the companion Skills, and provides a day-by-day Week One Checklist.

Appendix, Setup and Skill Installation Guide, provide step-by-step instructions for creating accounts, installing Skills, connecting integrations, customizing workflows, and troubleshooting.

To get the most out of this book

- You will need a free account on at least one AI tool (Claude, ChatGPT, or Perplexity). The book recommends Claude as the primary tool because of its strong reasoning, file handling, and integration capabilities, but every workflow works across tools.
- A Google account (for Gmail, Calendar, and Drive integrations) is recommended but not strictly required. If your organization uses Microsoft 365, the workflows apply but the integration setup differs. Check the Appendix for guidance.
- Paid tiers are helpful but not necessary. You can follow every workflow using free tiers. Upgrading to Claude Pro or ChatGPT Plus removes friction (higher limits, file uploads, more integrations) but is not required to learn or use the workflows.

Download the example code files

The code bundle for the book is hosted on GitHub at `https://github.com/PacktPublishing/AI-For-Everyday-Automation`. We also have other code bundles from our rich catalog of books and videos available at `https://github.com/PacktPublishing`. Check them out!

Conventions used

There are a number of text conventions used throughout this book.

`CodeInText`: Indicates AI prompts, folder names, filenames, file extensions, pathnames, dummy URLs, and user input. For example: "The power is in the follow-up: `make it shorter`, `change the opening`, `add a section on risks`."

Longer prompts are set in blocks as follows:

```
I have rough notes that need to become a polished [type: status update /
proposal / client summary / internal memo]. The audience is [who will read this].
```

Bold: Indicates a new term, an important word, or words that you see on the screen. For instance, words in menus or dialog boxes appear in the text like this. For example: "Look for the **Connectors** icon near the input box or in settings."

> Note
>
> Warnings or important notes appear like this.

> Tip
>
> Tips and tricks appear like this.

Get in touch

Feedback from our readers is always welcome.

General feedback: If you have questions about any aspect of this book or have any general feedback, please email us at `customercare@packt.com` and mention the book's title in the subject of your message.

Errata: Although we have taken every care to ensure the accuracy of our content, mistakes do happen. If you have found a mistake in this book, we would be grateful if you reported this to us. Please visit `https://www.packt.com/submit-errata`, click **Submit Errata**, and fill in the form.

Piracy: If you come across any illegal copies of our works in any form on the internet, we would be grateful if you would provide us with the location address or website name. Please contact us at `copyright@packt.com` with a link to the material.

If you are interested in becoming an author: If there is a topic that you have expertise in and you are interested in either writing or contributing to a book, please visit `https://authors.packt.com/`.

Free benefits with your book

This book comes with free benefits to support your learning. Activate them now for instant access (see the "*How to Unlock*" section for instructions).

Here's a quick overview of what you can instantly unlock with your purchase:

EPUB PDF

DRM-Free PDF Version

Download DRM-free PDF and ePub copies of this book.

7-Day Packt Library Access

Get 7-day unlimited access to 8,000+ books and videos. No credit card required.

Available for first-time Packt+ trial users only.

Next-Gen Reader Access

Read this book on Packt Reader with progress sync, dark mode and note-taking.

How to Unlock

Scan the QR code (or go to packtpub.com/unlock). Search for this book by name, confirm the edition, and then follow the steps on the page.

UNLOCK NOW

Note: Keep your invoice handy. Purchases made directly from Packt don't require one

Share your thoughts

Once you've read *AI for Everyday Automation*, we'd love to hear your thoughts! Scan the QR code below to go straight to the Amazon review page for this book and share your feedback.

`https://packt.link/r/1808089812`

Your review is important to us and the tech community and will help us make sure we're delivering excellent quality content.

1

Audit, Arm, Go

Most people who try AI at work follow the same pattern. They open ChatGPT, type a question, get an interesting answer, and then go back to doing things the way they always have. The problem is not that AI failed them but that they started without knowing what to point it at.

This chapter fixes that in a single sitting. You will do two things: first, identify exactly where your time goes and which tasks are worth automating; second, set up your AI tools so they know who you are, what you do, and how you communicate. When you finish this chapter, you will have a personal hit list and a loaded workbench. *Chapter 2* puts them together.

What you will achieve: By the end of this chapter, you will have identified the five tasks eating most of your week, set up three AI tools configured with your personal context, and be ready to automate your first workflow in *Chapter 2*.

> Note
>
> **Your purchase includes a free PDF copy + exclusive extras**
>
> Your purchase includes a DRM-free PDF copy of this book, 7-day trial to the Packt+ library (no credit card required), and additional exclusive extras. See the *Free benefits with your book* section in the *Preface* to unlock them instantly and maximize your learning.

Where your hours actually go

Before you automate anything, you need to know what you are automating and why. Rather than a detailed time-tracking exercise, this will be a fast, honest look at your week, producing a prioritized list of five tasks to target first.

The 30-minute time map

Open a blank document or a sheet of paper. Think through a typical work week; not your best week or your worst week, but the one that happens most often. List every recurring activity that takes more than 15 minutes. Don't worry about being precise. Rough estimates are fine. You are looking for patterns.

For each activity, write down three things:

1. **What you do**: One sentence. Example: "Read and respond to emails"
2. **How long it takes**: Per session and per week. Example: "30 minutes, three times a day, roughly 7–8 hours a week"
3. **How much of it is uniquely yours:** Could someone with your context but no special expertise handle 80% of it? If yes, it is a strong automation candidate.

Most knowledge workers find their weeks dominated by five categories: communication (email, Slack, messages), meetings (preparation, attendance, follow-up), research (finding and synthesizing information), document creation (reports, proposals, memos), and coordination (task tracking, status updates, chasing people). Your specific tasks will vary, but these categories cover the territory.

> Tip
>
> **Do not overthink this**
>
> The audit should take 20–30 minutes. If you spend more than that, you are optimizing the audit instead of doing it. A rough list you act on beats a perfect spreadsheet you never use.

Scoring your tasks: Time vs. cognitive uniqueness

Now score each task on two dimensions:

- **Time consumed:** How many hours per week does this task eat? Score it 1 (under an hour) to 5 (five or more hours).
- **Cognitive uniqueness**: How much of this task requires your specific judgment, creativity, or relationships? Score it 1 (almost none — anyone with context could do it) to 5 (deeply personal, requires your expertise).

The sweet spot for automation is tasks that score high on time consumed but low on cognitive uniqueness. These are the activities where you are spending hours on work that does not require your best thinking. Here's an example scoring matrix for common tasks:

Task	Time (1–5)	Uniqueness (1–5)	Automation potential
Email triage and replies	4–5	1–2	Very high — most replies follow patterns
Meeting follow-up notes	2–3	1–2	Very high — extraction from transcript
Competitive research	3–4	2–3	High — synthesis, not original analysis
Weekly status report	2–3	1–2	Very high — structured, repetitive format
Strategy presentation	3–4	4–5	Low — requires your strategic judgment
Client relationship calls	3–4	5	Very low — the relationship is the point

Table 1.1 - Example automation scoring matrix. Your tasks will differ, but the pattern holds: high time, low uniqueness = automate first

Building your hit list

From your scored list, pick the five tasks with the highest automation potential. These become your personal hit list for the rest of the book. Write them down somewhere you will see them. Each one maps to a chapter:

If your hit list includes...	Go to...
Email triage and drafting	*Chapter 3: Inbox Zero in 25 Minutes*
Meeting prep and follow-up	*Chapter 4: Meetings That Actually Work*
Research and intelligence gathering	*Chapter 5: Research in 30 Minutes*

If your hit list includes...	Go to...
Reports, proposals, memos	*Chapter 6: First Drafts in 15 Minutes*
Task tracking and coordination	*Chapter 7:* Tracked Tasks in 15 Minutes
Data cleaning and analysis	*Chapter 8: Spreadsheets Without* Writing Formulas
Content and communications	*Chapter 9:* Write Once, Use Everywhere

Table 1.2 - Hit list to chapter mapping. You do not need to read the book in order—start with whatever hurts most

You do not need to tackle all seven workflow chapters. Start with the two or three that match your biggest time sinks. You can always come back to the others.

While it is possible that your tasks are different from the above hit list, these categories represent the activities with the highest automation potential. In most cases, your specific tasks can be mapped back to a similar one from the list.

Setting up your AI workbench

You now know what to automate. The next step is configuring the tools that will do the work. This section gets you set up with three AI tools, each configured with your personal context, in under 30 minutes.

Why three tools, not one?

No single AI tool is best at everything. Rather than recommending thirty tools and overwhelming you, this book uses a focused stack of three, each chosen for a specific strength:

- **Claude** (`https://claude.ai`) by Anthropic is the primary tool for long-context work: analyzing documents, synthesizing transcripts, drafting reports, and any task where you need to feed in substantial context and get structured output back. Claude handles nuance and extended reasoning better than any other tool available today.
- **ChatGPT** (`https://chatgpt.com/`) by OpenAI has the broadest ecosystem: custom GPTs, a mobile app, plugins, and an Advanced Data Analysis mode that lets you upload spreadsheets and get cleaned data, charts, and summaries without writing code. Most readers already have an account, which removes friction.

- **Perplexity** (`https://www.perplexity.ai/`) is purpose-built for research. It searches the web and returns answers with inline source citations. When you need facts rather than drafts, Perplexity replaces the "Google for 30 minutes and hope" workflow.

> Note
>
> **Important: Tools are interchangeable**
>
> This book teaches workflows and prompt patterns, not brand loyalty. If you prefer Gemini over ChatGPT, or Copilot over Claude, the patterns transfer. The prompts in this book will work across any capable AI model with minor adjustments. All the tools in this case can be operated on the web and also have a companion desktop application that you can use.

Free vs. paid: What you actually need

You can follow every workflow in this book using free tiers. However, paid tiers remove friction in specific ways:

Tool	Free tier gives you	Paid tier adds
Claude	Limited messages per day, access to core model	Higher limits, file uploads, Projects for prompt management
ChatGPT	GPT-5 access, limited Advanced Data Analysis	Unlimited Advanced Data Analysis, custom GPTs, higher limits, image generation
Perplexity	Standard search with citations	Pro Search with deeper analysis, file uploads, and higher limits

Table 1.3 - Free vs. paid tier comparison. Start free. Upgrade when you hit the limits, not before

I recommend that you start with free tiers for all three tools. Work through the book for a week. If you find yourself hitting rate limits regularly, upgrade the tool you use the most. For most readers, one paid subscription (Claude Pro or ChatGPT Plus) is sufficient.

You do not need to agonize over tool selection for every task. Most of the model providers upgrade their models. Here is a simple decision framework based on available models at the time of print:

When you need to...	Reach for...	Because...
Analyze a long document, transcript, or dataset	Claude	Best long-context reasoning
Draft an email, report, or memo	Claude	Best at nuanced, voice-aware writing
Clean, chart, or analyze a spreadsheet	ChatGPT	Advanced Data Analysis sandbox
Build a reusable workflow (custom GPT)	ChatGPT	GPT Builder ecosystem
Research a topic with sourced facts	Perplexity	Inline citations, web-sourced
Quick question while mobile	ChatGPT or Claude app	Best mobile experience

Table 1.4 - Tool decision framework. Start here and adjust as you develop preferences

Teaching your tools who you are

The single most important setup step is configuring **custom instructions**. This is the difference between AI that gives you generic answers and AI that gives you answers tailored to your role, communication style, and context.

Custom instructions are a persistent prompt that runs behind every conversation. You write them once and the AI applies them automatically. Think of them as briefing a new colleague on your first day: here is what I do, here is how I communicate, and here is what I care about.

> **Note**
>
> It is important to be aware of the terms and conditions of the AI services that you use. Most platforms, when used on free plans, will use your data to train their models. When working with private data, do review your organization's data security and privacy policies to ensure that you are not violating them.

A good custom instruction covers four areas:

1. **Your role and context:** What is your job title? What industry? What team size? Example: `I am a product manager at a B2B SaaS company with a team of 8.`
2. **Your communication style:** Are you direct or diplomatic? Do you use bullet points or prose? Formal or casual? Example: `I write in a direct, concise style. I prefer bullet points for internal communication and polished prose for client-facing work.`
3. **Your common tasks:** What do you ask AI to help with most often? Example: `I frequently draft emails, summarize meeting transcripts, and create weekly status reports.`
4. **Your preferences:** Any recurring instructions you find yourself repeating? Example: `Always use US English spellings. Keep emails under 150 words unless I say otherwise.`

> **Tip**
>
> **Start simple, iterate later**
>
> Your first custom instruction does not need to be perfect. Write 3–5 sentences covering your role and style. You will refine it over the first week as you discover what produces the best results.

Example custom instruction

Here is a starter custom instruction you can adapt. Replace the bracketed sections with your own details:

```
I am a [job title] at a [industry/company type] company. My team has [number]
people. I report to [role].
```

```
I write in a [direct/diplomatic] style. I prefer [bullet points/prose] for
internal communication and [polished prose/structured format] for client-facing
work.

I frequently need help with: [list 3-5 common tasks, e.g., drafting emails,
summarizing meetings, writing status reports].

Use [UK/US] English. Be concise.
```

Set this up in each tool. In Claude, go to the **General** tab under **Settings** and find the field called **Instructions for Claude**. In ChatGPT, go to **Settings** > **Personalization** > **Custom Instructions**. The exact location may vary as interfaces update, but the concept is the same everywhere: a persistent prompt that shapes every response.

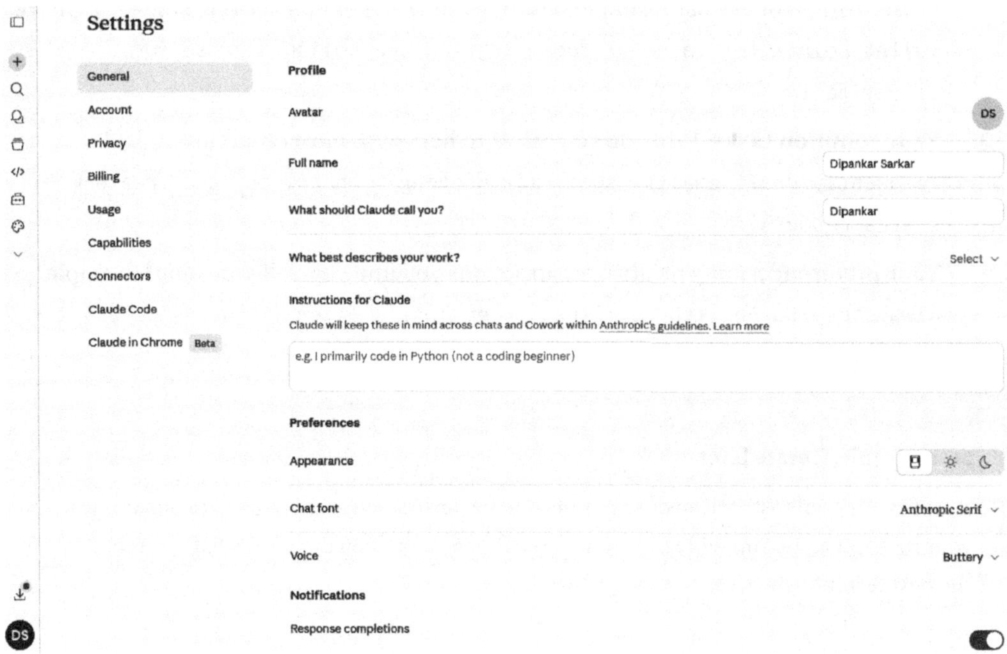

Figure 1.1 – You can input your custom instructions under the General profile settings in Claude

Verifying everything works

Before moving to *Chapter 2*, run this simple test in each tool to confirm your setup is working. Open a new conversation and type:

```
Based on what you know about me and my role, draft a 3-sentence introduction I
could use at a professional event.
```

If your custom instructions are working, the response should reflect your job title, industry, and communication style without you having to repeat any of that context. If it gives you a generic response, your custom instructions are not set up correctly — go back and check.

> Tip
>
> **Save this as a diagnostic**
>
> Whenever you update your custom instructions, re-run this smoke test. It is the fastest way to check whether the AI has absorbed your context correctly.

Summary

You have accomplished two things in this chapter:

1. **A personal hit list** of five tasks that consume your time without requiring your best thinking. These are your automation targets.
2. **A configured workbench** of three AI tools that know who you are, what you do, and how you communicate.

In *Chapter 2*, you will put them together. You will pick one task from your hit list, complete it with AI assistance in under 30 minutes, and experience the full workflow loop: input, prompt, review, use.

Time to move. Turn to *Chapter 2* and do your first AI-assisted task.

Get this book's PDF version and more

Scan the QR code (or go to `packtpub.com/unlock`). Search for this book by name, confirm the edition, and then follow the steps on the page.

UNLOCK NOW

Note: Keep your invoice handy. Purchases made directly from Packt don't require an invoice.

2

Your First AI Win

You have your hit list and tools. This chapter is where you stop reading about AI productivity and start doing it.

The goal is deliberately small. You will pick one task, do it with AI right now, and finish this chapter having saved time on real work. Rather than toy examples or practice prompts, this chapter equips you to tackle a task from your actual job.

Why start with one task instead of diving into the full workflow chapters? Because the biggest barrier to AI adoption is not knowledge; it is the gap between knowing AI could help and actually using it on a Tuesday afternoon when you have fourteen unread emails and a report due by end of day. This chapter closes that gap.

What you will achieve: By the end of this chapter, you will have completed one real task with AI assistance in under 30 minutes and experienced the full workflow loop: gather input, write a prompt, review AI output, refine it, and use the result.

> Note
>
> **How to use this chapter**
>
> Pick one of the three walkthroughs below based on your hit list from *Chapter 1*. Each walkthrough takes 20–30 minutes and produces a real, usable output. You only need to do one.

Walkthrough 1: Batch-draft three email replies

In this walkthrough, we will learn how to use AI for email triage, response drafting, and managing your inbox.

Step 1: Gather your inputs

Open your inbox. Find three emails that need replies but are not urgent enough to have answered yet. These are the emails that sit for a day or two because replying feels effortful but not important enough to prioritize. Copy the text of all three into a single document or note.

For each email, add one line at the top noting your intent:

- What is the key thing you need to communicate?
- What is the tone? (e.g., "friendly decline," "confirm and ask a follow-up," "say yes but set a boundary")

Step 2: Write the prompt

Open Claude (or your preferred tool). Paste the following prompt, replacing the bracketed sections:

```
I need to reply to three emails. For each one, I have pasted the original email
and a note about my intended response. Please draft all three replies in my voice
(refer to my custom instructions for style).

Keep each reply under 150 words unless the situation demands more. Match the
formality level of the original email.
---
EMAIL 1:
[paste the email]
MY INTENT: [one sentence, e.g., "Decline the meeting but suggest an async
alternative"]
---
EMAIL 2:
[paste the email]
MY INTENT: [one sentence]
---
EMAIL 3:
[paste the email]
MY INTENT: [one sentence]
```

Step 3: Review the output

The AI will return three drafted replies. Read each one and ask yourself two questions:

- **Does it say what I need it to say?** Check that the core message matches your intent. If the AI missed your point, that is a prompt problem.
- **Does it sound like me?** If the tone is off, this is a signal that your custom instructions need refining. Note what feels wrong for later.

Step 4: Refine with a follow-up

If any reply needs adjustment, do not rewrite it manually. Instead, tell the AI what to change:

```
Reply 2 is too formal. Make it warmer and more casual. Also, add a line
acknowledging their timeline concern.
```

This is the key habit the book will build: use follow-up prompts to steer, do not revert to writing from scratch. Every follow-up prompt teaches you to communicate with AI more precisely, which makes every subsequent task faster.

Step 5: Use the result

Copy the final replies into your email client. Make any last tweaks (you are always the final editor), and send. You have just processed three emails that would have sat in your inbox for another day.

> Tip
>
> **Time yourself**
>
> Check how long this took. Most readers report 10–15 minutes for three emails, compared to 20–30 minutes of drafting manually. The savings compound as you develop your prompting instincts.

Walkthrough 2: Summarize a recent meeting

In this walkthrough, we will learn to use AI to generate meeting follow-up, take notes, and track action items.

Step 1: Gather your inputs

Find the notes or transcript from your most recent meeting. This could be:

- A transcript from AI-based transcription tools like Otter.ai, Fireflies, or your video conferencing tool's built-in transcription

- Your own handwritten or typed notes
- A Slack thread or email chain that served as the meeting's context

If you do not have a transcript, use your best meeting notes. Even rough notes produce useful output.

> **Note**
>
> Most transcription services make export straightforward. Whether you're using a dedicated transcription app or built-in platform transcription, the workflow is broadly the same: open the meeting or conversation, find the export or share option, and download a plain text or document file. The format details matter less than you might think — the AI does not need timestamps or speaker-labelled formatting to produce a good summary, though those details improve the quality of action item attribution if they are available. If your tool offers multiple export formats, prefer plain text or a standard document format over proprietary ones; if it only offers copy-to-clipboard, that works too.
>
> Specific guidelines for common tools at the time of writing:
>
> - **Otter.ai**: Open the conversation from your dashboard and use the export or share option to download as a text file.
>
> - **Fireflies.ai**: Navigate to the meeting in your notebook and export the transcript.
>
> - **Zoom**: Transcripts are saved alongside your cloud recordings in the Zoom web portal.
>
> - **Google Meet**: When transcription is enabled, transcripts appear as Google Docs in your Drive.
>
> - **Microsoft Teams**: Transcripts are stored in the meeting chat or the recap tab.

Step 2: Write the prompt

Paste your notes or transcript into Claude or ChatGPT along with this prompt:

```
Here are my notes from a meeting. Please produce a structured summary with the
following sections:

1. KEY DECISIONS: What was decided? List each decision as a single clear sentence.

2. ACTION ITEMS: For each action item, include:
   - What needs to be done
   - Who is responsible (use names from the transcript)
```

```
   - Deadline (if mentioned; otherwise mark as TBD)

3. OPEN QUESTIONS: What was raised but not resolved?

4. SUMMARY: A 3-5 sentence overview of the meeting, suitable for sharing with
someone who was not there.

[Paste your meeting notes/transcript here]
```

Step 3: Review the output

Check the output against your memory of the meeting. The most common issues are:

- **Misattributed action items**: The AI may guess who is responsible if the transcript is ambiguous. Correct these.
- **Missing context**: If something important was said off-mic or in chat, it will not appear. Add it manually.
- **Overly cautious summary**: The AI may hedge where you would be more direct. Tighten the language.

Step 4: Refine with a follow-up

You can reply to the chat with a follow-up to correct the summary as shown here:

```
The action item about the Q3 timeline should be assigned to Sarah, not James.
Also, add a decision that we agreed to postpone the vendor evaluation until after
the board meeting.
```

Step 5: Use the result

Copy the structured summary and share it with meeting attendees via email or Slack. This is now your meeting record. In *Chapter 4*, you will learn how to make this automatic for every meeting.

Notice what just happened: a task that normally takes 20–30 minutes of post-meeting writing is now a 5-minute review. The AI did the structural work. You did the quality control.

Walkthrough 3: Turn bullet points into a polished memo

In this walkthrough, you will learn to use AI for report writing, document drafting, and internal communications.

Step 1: Gather your inputs

Find a set of rough notes, bullet points, or scattered thoughts for something you need to write. This could be:

- A weekly status update you have been meaning to send
- Notes for a project proposal
- Bullet points from a client conversation that need to become a summary email
- Data or observations that need to become a one-page internal memo

The rougher the input, the more dramatic the result. Do not polish your notes before feeding them to AI. That defeats the purpose.

Step 2: Write the prompt

You should try the following prompt and replace the square bracket items with your choices and relevant details in Claude or ChatGPT. Always make sure that the data you share is not violating any relevant data privacy policies.

```
I have rough notes that need to become a polished [type: status update /
proposal / client summary / internal memo]. The audience is [who will read this].

Please:
1. Organize the information logically
2. Write in a professional, [concise/detailed] style
3. Keep it to [one page / 300 words / 5 paragraphs]
4. Highlight any gaps where I may need to add information

Here are my rough notes:
[Paste your bullet points / notes here]
```

Step 3: Review the output

The AI will produce a structured document from your rough notes. Check for:

- **Accuracy**: Did it invent any facts that were not in your notes? This is the most important check. If numbers, dates, or claims appear that you did not provide, delete them.
- **Structure**: Does the organization make sense? Would you rearrange any sections?
- **Tone**: Does it match what the audience expects? A board memo and a Slack update need very different registers.

Step 4: Refine with a follow-up

After the review you can reply with the changes that you want like this example follow-up prompt:

```
Good structure. Two changes:
(1) the opening paragraph should lead with the key recommendation, not the
background context.
(2) Add a section at the end titled "Next Steps" with three specific actions.
```

Again, notice the pattern: you are directing, not drafting. The AI handles the structural and linguistic heavy lifting. You handle accuracy and judgment.

Step 5: Use the result

Review the results and do more follow-ups as needed. Copy the final document into your preferred medium (email, Google Docs, Notion, Slack) and send it. A memo that might have taken 45 minutes of staring at a blank page is done in 15 minutes.

What just happened

Whichever walkthrough you chose, you have now experienced the fundamental loop that powers every workflow in this book:

1. **Gather input**: collect the raw material (emails, transcripts, notes, data)
2. **Write a structured prompt**: tell the AI what you need, with format and constraints
3. **Review the output**: check for accuracy, tone, and completeness
4. **Refine with follow-ups**: steer, do not rewrite
5. **Use the result**: send, share, or publish

Every chapter that follows applies this same loop to a specific task domain, with deeper prompts, multi-step chains, and reusable templates. But the loop itself does not change. You have already learned the core skill.

> Note
>
> **The habit that matters the most**
>
> The single most valuable habit from this chapter is *Step 4*: refining with follow-up prompts instead of reverting to manual editing. This is what separates people who use AI occasionally from people who use AI as daily infrastructure. Every follow-up prompt makes you a better AI collaborator.

Three lessons to carry forward

If you have done the exercises in the previous sections, you are well on your way toward making the best use of automation coming up in the following chapters. Here are the key lessons that we will continue to apply as we go forward.

Lesson 1: Imperfect input is fine

You do not need to prepare your inputs before giving them to AI. Messy notes, incomplete transcripts, and rough bullet points all produce useful output. The AI is better at imposing structure on chaos than you are at pre-structuring chaos before asking for help. Feed it the mess.

Lesson 2: A prompt is a conversation, not a command

Your first prompt will rarely produce the perfect output. That is expected. The power is in the follow-up prompts, such as `make it shorter`, `change the opening`, and `add a section on risks`. Treat the AI like a fast, tireless first-drafter who takes direction well. The better your direction, the better the output.

Lesson 3: Be the editor, not the writer

The mental shift this book will build is from writer to editor. Writers stare at blank pages. Editors shape existing material. When you use AI for the first draft, you skip the hardest part of every writing task (starting) and go straight to the part humans do best (judging quality, catching errors, refining tone). *Chapters 3* through *9* will deepen this shift across every domain of your work.

Summary

In this chapter, you learned the core AI workflow loop and applied it to one real-world task: email drafting, meeting summarization, or memo creation.

You have your first win. You know the loop. Now it is time to go deep.

Look at your hit list from *Chapter 1*. Find the task that costs you the most time and turn to the corresponding chapter. You do not need to read the chapters in order. Each one is self-contained, with its own prompts, templates, and worked examples. Start where the pain is greatest.

1. *Chapter 3: Inbox Zero in 25 Minutes* — full email triage and drafting system
2. *Chapter 4: Meetings That Actually Work* — automated prep, transcription, and follow-up
3. *Chapter 5: Research in 30 Minutes, Not 3 Hours* — sourced research briefs

4. *Chapter 6*: *First Drafts in 15 Minutes* — document generation chains
5. *Chapter 7*: *Tracked Tasks in 15 Minutes* — task extraction and coordination
6. *Chapter 8*: *Spreadsheets Without Writing Formulas* — data cleaning and analysis
7. *Chapter 9*: *Write Once, Use Everywhere* — multi-format content creation

Pick your chapter. Let's go.

Get this book's PDF version and more

Scan the QR code (or go to `packtpub.com/unlock`). Search for this book by name, confirm the edition, and then follow the steps on the page.

UNLOCK NOW

Note: Keep your invoice handy. Purchases made directly from Packt don't require an invoice.

3

Inbox Zero in 25 Minutes

In *Chapter 2*, you completed a task with AI by copying an email, pasting it into Claude, and copying the reply back out. That worked. But if you do it forty times a day, the copy-paste overhead adds up fast.

This chapter introduces the idea that powers the rest of the book: connecting your AI tool directly to the services you use. When Claude can read your Gmail inbox, it does not need you to paste emails. The AI reads and drafts emails,. You review, approve and send.

Email is the ideal place to learn this pattern because it is high volume, low stakes per message, and immediately familiar. Once you see connected AI working on email, applying it to meetings (*Chapter 4*), research (*Chapter 5*), and documents (*Chapter 6*) will feel natural.

What you will achieve: You will connect your Gmail to Claude, let it read and classify your inbox and draft replies in your voice — all without leaving the conversation. By the end of this chapter, email becomes a 25-minute batch process rather than an all-day interruption.

> Note
>
> **What are integrations?**
>
> AI tools like Claude and ChatGPT can now connect to external services — your calendar, email, task manager, cloud storage — through **connectors** (sometimes called MCP servers, plugins, or integrations). Once connected, the AI can read your calendar events, search your Google Drive, create tasks in Asana, and more, all within the same conversation. You set up the connection once and it persists across sessions.

Setting up the integrations

Both Claude and ChatGPT support connections to external services. The setup takes 5–10 minutes per service and only needs to be done once.

In Claude

Claude connects to external tools through its **Connectors** panel. At the time of writing, Claude supports direct connections to Google Calendar, Google Drive, Gmail, and a growing list of third-party services. To connect:

1. Open a new conversation in Claude
2. Look for the **Connectors** icon near the input box or in settings
3. Select the service you want to connect (e.g., Google Calendar)
4. Authorize Claude to access your account. You will be redirected to the service's login page.
5. Once connected, Claude can read from and interact with that service in any conversation

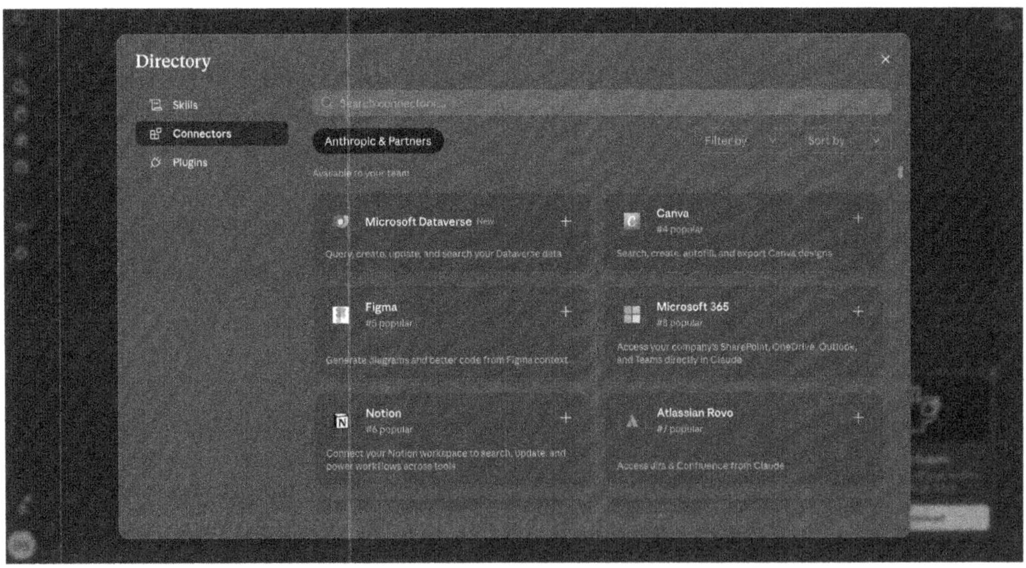

Figure 3.1 – Claude Connectors Settings Panel

In ChatGPT

ChatGPT connects through plugins, custom GPTs, and increasingly through MCP-compatible integrations. Many calendar and task management services are available. Users can browse and enable these from the **Apps** section in the left sidebar, which lists available integrations and shows which ones are already connected. From there, it's a matter of selecting the service, authorizing access through the standard OAuth flow, and the integration becomes available in chat. The pattern is the same across services: enable the integration, authorize access, and ChatGPT can then read from and write to the service.

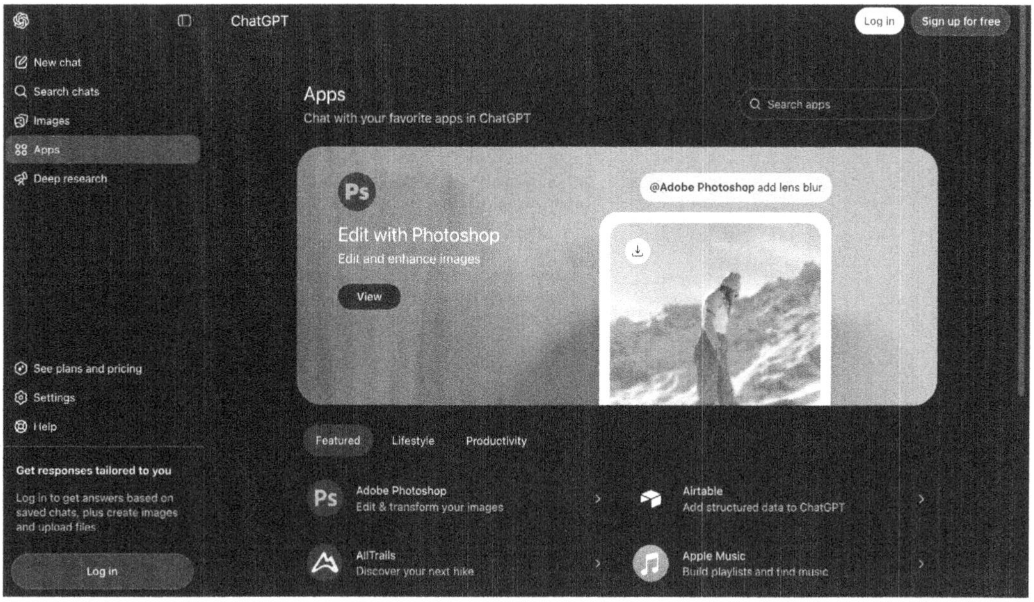

Figure 3.2 – ChatGPT Apps Section

The connected email workflow

The workflow runs in batch as you process your inbox in a single focused session. With Gmail connected, the four stages — classify, draft, review, approve — all happen inside one AI conversation.

Stage 1: Let the AI classify your inbox

Instead of scanning your inbox manually, ask the AI to do the triage:

```
Read my Gmail inbox. Show me all unread emails from the past 24 hours. For each
one, classify it as:
1. ACT NOW — needs my response today
2. ACT LATER — needs a response but not urgently
3. INFORM ONLY — no response needed, just awareness
```

```
For each email, show: sender, subject, your classification, and a one-sentence
summary of what they need from me (if anything).
```

The AI reads your inbox, scans every unread email, and returns a classified list. What used to take 10–15 minutes of scanning and deciding now takes 30 seconds of reading a structured summary. You review the classifications, override any the AI got wrong, and move to *Stage 2* with a clean, prioritized list.

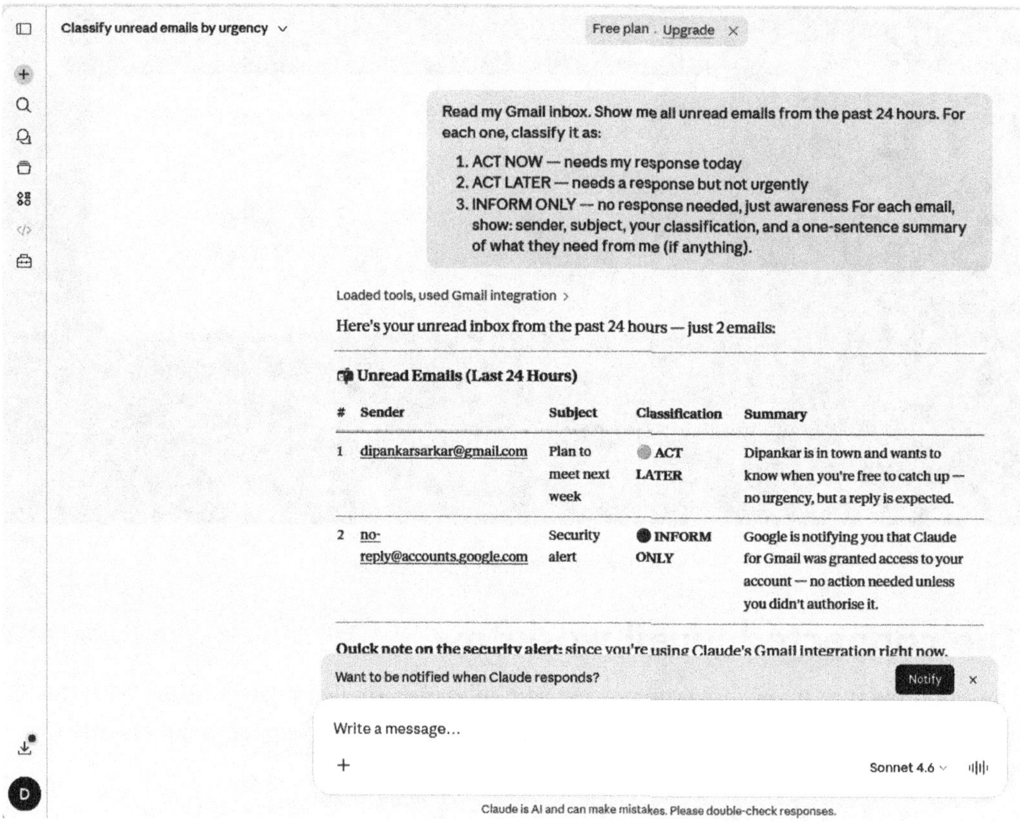

Figure 3.3 – Claude Session classifying a Gmail inbox

Stage 2: Batch-draft replies

Now tell the AI to draft replies for your "Act Now" queue:

```
For each ACT NOW email, draft a reply. My intent for each:
1. [Sender/subject] – [your intent, e.g., "Confirm but move the time to 3pm"]
2. [Sender/subject] – [intent]
3. [Sender/subject] – [intent]
```

```
Guidelines:
- Keep each reply under 150 words unless the situation demands more
- Match the formality level of the original sender
- Refer to my custom instructions for voice and style
```

Because the AI has already read the emails in *Stage 1*, it has full context. You do not need to paste anything. Just provide your intent for each reply—one sentence per email—and the AI drafts all of them at once.

The intent note is the key to good drafts. "Decline politely" produces a generic decline. "Decline the meeting but suggest an async Loom video instead because the topic is straightforward" produces a reply that sounds like you thought about it. Specificity in intent produces quality in output.

Stage 3: Review and refine

The AI presents each draft. Read them and check three things:

- **Accuracy**: Does it say what you intended? If the AI missed your point, note it for a follow-up.
- **Tone**: Does it sound like you? If the voice is off, refine your voice guide (covered later in this chapter).
- **Completeness**: Did the AI skip a question from the original email?

For drafts that need adjustment, you can use a prompt like this:

```
Reply 2 needs changes:
- Too apologetic. Remove the apology, lead with the decision.
- Add a line acknowledging their timeline pressure.
- Warmer closing – this is a long-term client.
```

Most replies need zero or one adjustment. The goal is not zero edits but less time than writing from scratch.

Stage 4: Approve and click send

This is where connected AI saves the most time. Instead of copying each draft back into Gmail, use this prompt:

```
The drafts look good. Please draft replies 1, 2, and 3 via Gmail. For reply 4,
hold – I want to edit that one manually before sending.
```

The AI creates the draft for you on Gmail without requiring any copying, pasting, or switching windows. For any reply you want to edit further, tell the AI to hold it and either refine it with another follow-up prompt or open Gmail to edit manually.

> Note
>
> **You are always the final gate**
>
> Connected AI only drafts on your behalf. The job gets done when you check and click send. The AI will show you every draft and wait for your go-ahead. You can approve all, approve selectively, or hold everything for manual review. The control is yours.

The single-prompt morning workflow

Once you are comfortable with the four stages, you can compress them into a single morning prompt:

```
Good morning. Please:

1. Read my Gmail inbox — all unread emails from the past 24 hours
2. Classify each as ACT NOW / ACT LATER / INFORM ONLY
3. For ACT NOW emails, draft replies using my voice guide and custom instructions
4. Present the classified list with draft replies for my review

I will provide specific intent for any email where a generic reply is not
appropriate. For routine emails (meeting confirmations, simple acknowledgements,
straightforward information requests), draft a sensible reply based on the
content.
```

This prompt runs the entire email workflow in one shot. The AI reads your inbox, classifies everything, and pre-drafts replies for the urgent items. You review, provide intent for anything that needs a specific response, refine any drafts, and sned. Total time: 20–25 minutes for a full inbox.

Some readers run this prompt every morning at 9 AM and every afternoon at 3 PM. Two sessions, 25 minutes each, and email is handled for the entire day.

Building your voice guide

The most common complaint about AI-drafted emails is "it does not sound like me." This is solvable. The solution is a **voice guide**: a short document describing how you write, with examples that you include in your custom instructions.

How to write your voice guide

A voice guide has three sections:

1. **General rules**: 3–5 sentences. Example: `I write in short, direct sentences. I avoid corporate jargon. I use contractions. I open with the key point, not pleasantries.`
2. **Audience adjustments**: How your style shifts. Example: `To my team: casual, bullet points fine. To clients: professional but warm. To executives: extremely concise, lead with the ask.`
3. **Examples**: 2–3 emails you have actually sent that represent your voice. These are the most powerful part — they give the AI concrete patterns rather than abstract rules.

Here's a sample structure for your voice guide:

```
VOICE GUIDE

General: Short sentences, active voice, no filler phrases like "I just wanted to"
or "I hope this finds you well." I use contractions. Direct but not blunt - I
acknowledge the other person's perspective before stating mine.

To my team: Casual. First names. Bullets are fine.
To clients: Professional, warm. Full sentences.
To leadership: Extremely concise. Lead with the ask.

EXAMPLES:
[paste 2-3 emails you have sent that represent your
voice well]
```

Paste this into your custom instructions (*Chapter 1*) so it applies to every conversation. The voice guide improves with use — every time you notice the AI getting something wrong, add a rule.

Tip

Teach by correcting

When you refine a draft ("make it warmer," "remove the apology"), those corrections are teaching material. After a week, review your corrections and add the patterns to your voice guide. "Never open with a thank-you for their email" is a rule that saves you from correcting the same thing every session.

Five email prompt templates

These templates cover roughly 80% of professional email. With Gmail connected, you reference emails by sender and subject rather than pasting content.

You can use these as ways to get better responses or outcomes from the AI.

Template 1: Decline a meeting or request

The following prompt will draft a response:

```
Read the email from [sender] about [subject]. Draft a reply declining [the
meeting / the request]. Be warm but clear. Suggest [an alternative: async update /
different time / delegating to someone]. Keep it under 100 words. Do not include
my real reason for declining.
```

Template 2: Follow up on a deliverable

You can use the following prompt to write a follow-up:

```
Read the thread with [person] about [deliverable].
The original deadline was [date]. Draft a follow-up that is [friendly / direct /
urgent] and under 100 words.
Context: [e.g., "this is the second follow-up" or "they are usually reliable"].
```

Template 3: Request information or action

This is an example prompt for writing out the request:

```
Draft an email to [person] requesting [specific thing]. Make the ask crystal clear
– they should know exactly what to do after reading. Deadline: [date]. Under 120
words.
Context: [why you need it].
```

Template 4: Status update

This is a prompt for writing a status update:

```
Draft a status update email for [project].
Audience:[who reads this].
Structure: (1) one-sentence overall status, (2) key progress (2-3 bullets), (3)
blockers, (4) next steps.

Pull context from:
- My recent emails about [project] in Gmail
- [Any other source, e.g., "the meeting packet from Thursday in my Drive"]
```

Template 5: Handle a complaint or difficult message

This is a prompt that helps you handle difficult responses.

```
Read the email from [sender] about [subject]. This is a complaint. Draft a reply
that acknowledges their frustration without being defensive. My goal: [resolve the
issue / acknowledge and buy time / redirect].

What I can offer: [the real resolution]
What I cannot say: [e.g., "don't admit fault" or "don't promise a date"]
```

When to write manually

Not every email should be AI-drafted, and not every email should go through a connected tool:

- **Performance feedback** (positive or negative): The personal nuance matters too much
- **Conflict resolution**: Subtle miscalibration in tone can escalate rather than resolve
- **Confidential or legally sensitive content**: Check your organization's data policies on what can be shared with AI tools
- **Relationship-critical messages**: When the email itself is the relationship work

The rule of thumb: if getting the tone wrong by 10% would cause real damage, write it yourself.

> Note
>
> **Data privacy with connected Gmail**
>
> When Claude reads your Gmail, email content is processed through Anthropic's servers. Most AI providers do not train on your data, but the content does leave your device. If your emails contain sensitive personal data, financial information, or material subject to regulatory requirements (GDPR, HIPAA, financial regulations), check your organization's policy before connecting Gmail. When in doubt, use the manual copy-paste workflow for sensitive threads and the connected workflow for routine correspondence.

Advanced: Processing complex threads

Long email threads with multiple participants are where connected AI saves the most cognitive effort. Instead of reading a 20-message thread to figure out what is being asked of you, use this prompt:

```
Read the email thread with [participants] about [subject]. This thread has gotten
long. Please:
1. Summarize the thread: what is the core question or decision being discussed?
2. What is each person's position?
3. What is being asked of me specifically?
4. What is unresolved?

Then draft my reply. My intent: [your one-sentence intent]. Address each
unresolved point. Under 200 words. Use names.
```

The AI reads the entire thread directly from Gmail, summarizes it, and drafts your reply, all without you reading 20 messages. You review the summary to make sure it is accurate, approve or refine the draft, and send. A thread that would take 15 minutes of careful reading becomes 3 minutes of review.

The daily rhythm

The connected email workflow works best on a fixed schedule:

Session	Time	What happens
Morning	9:00–9:25 AM	Run the single-prompt workflow. AI reads inbox, classifies, drafts, you review and send.
Midday check	12:30 PM (2 min)	Quick scan using the templates for urgent items only. Do not draft unless it is truly time-sensitive.
Afternoon	3:00–3:20 PM	Second full workflow. Process the *Act Later* queue from morning plus new arrivals.
End of day	5:30 PM (2 min)	Final scan. Anything that cannot wait until morning gets a quick reply.

Table 3.1: Daily email rhythm. Two connected AI sessions plus two quick checks replace all-day inbox monitoring

The key discipline: do not check email outside these windows. Every mid-session dip costs a context switch. Two focused sessions give you approximately five hours of uninterrupted deep work while maintaining responsive turnaround.

> Tip
>
> **Set expectations**
>
> Tell your team: "I process email at 9 AM and 3 PM. If something is truly urgent, message me on Slack." This sets expectations and prevents anyone from thinking you are ignoring them.

Fallback: When Gmail cannot be connected

If your organization restricts AI integrations with email, the workflow still works with manual steps:

1. **Classify manually** by scanning your inbox and starring or labelling the *Act Now* emails
2. **Copy the Act Now emails** and paste them into Claude with your intent notes (the *Chapter 2* approach)
3. **Copy the drafts back** into Gmail and send them manually

The prompts are identical. The only difference is the copy-paste overhead, which adds 5–10 minutes to each session. Start here if you need to and add the Gmail connection when your organization permits it.

Summary

In this chapter you have completed the following:

- **A connected email workflow** where AI reads your Gmail, classifies emails, and drafts replies in your voice
- **A single morning prompt** that runs the entire workflow: read, classify, draft, and review
- **A voice guide** that keeps AI drafts sounding like you, improving with every correction
- **Five connected templates** for the most common email types, referencing emails by sender and subject rather than copy-pasting
- **A daily rhythm** of two focused sessions replacing all-day inbox monitoring
- **A fallback workflow** for environments where Gmail integration is not available

This chapter introduced the connected AI pattern: instead of copy-pasting data between your tools and your AI, you connect them. The AI reads from your tools, processes the information, and writes back to them. You review and approve. This is the pattern that powers every chapter going forward.

We will apply this pattern to meetings in *Chapter 4* — connecting your calendar, transcription, and task tools so that meeting briefs generate automatically and action items are pushed directly to your project tracker.

Get this book's PDF version and more

Scan the QR code (or go to `packtpub.com/unlock`). Search for this book by name, confirm the edition, and then follow the steps on the page.

UNLOCK NOW

Note: Keep your invoice handy. Purchases made directly from Packt don't require an invoice.

4

Meetings That Actually Work

In *Chapter 3*, you used a connected workflow to turn email into a focused batch process. Meetings follow the same pattern, but the payoff is even larger. Every meeting generates a trail of work: preparing context beforehand, capturing notes during the discussion, summarizing decisions afterward, assigning action items, and tracking follow-ups. Most of that effort happens outside the meeting itself.

This chapter shows how to connect those pieces into a single workflow. Your calendar provides context, your transcription tool captures the conversation, and your AI assistant turns the discussion into summaries, decisions, and actionable next steps. Instead of rebuilding the story of the meeting afterward, you review and refine outputs that are already prepared for you.

The result is a meeting process where preparation, documentation, and follow-up happen automatically, allowing you to focus on the conversation itself.

What you will achieve: You will connect your calendar, transcription service, and task tools to your AI so that meeting briefs generate automatically, transcripts flow in without copy-pasting, and action items push directly to your project tracker.

The connected meeting stack

The automated meeting workflow uses four connected layers:

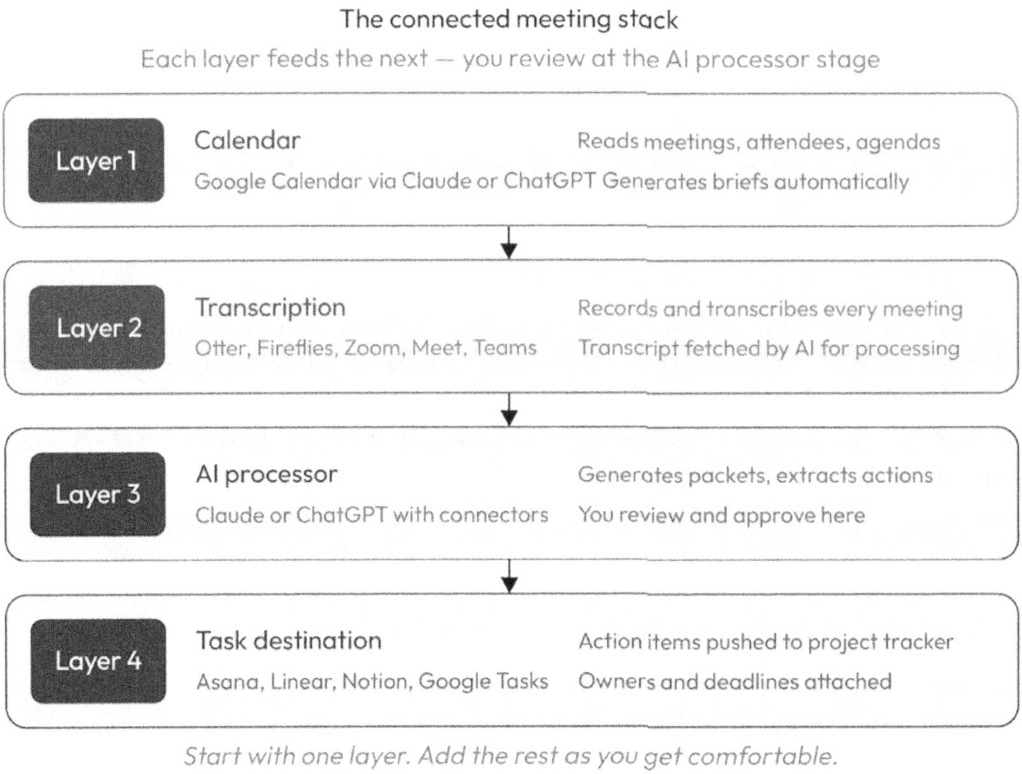

Figure 4.1 – The connected meeting stack. Each layer feeds the next. You review at the AI processor stage

You do not need all four layers to start. Even connecting just your calendar transforms meeting preparation. Add layers as you get comfortable.

You can follow the same email connection introduced in *Chapter 3*. You will see most of the above tools in the available integrations list.

Tip

Start with calendar, add the rest later

If connecting multiple services feels overwhelming, start with just your calendar. That single connection unlocks automated pre-meeting briefs, which is the highest-impact feature in this chapter. Add transcription and task integrations once the calendar workflow is running smoothly.

Before the meeting: Automated briefs

With your calendar connected, the AI generates pre-meeting briefs without you pasting anything:

```
What meetings do I have in the next 2 hours? For each one, generate a pre-meeting
brief with:
1. CONTEXT: What is this meeting about based on the calendar invite and any
attached documents?
2. KEY PEOPLE: Who is attending and what is their likely perspective?
3. MY PREP: What should I review or be ready to discuss?
4. OPEN ITEMS: If I have notes from a previous meeting with this group, what was
left unresolved?
```

Because the AI has access to your calendar, it pulls the meeting title, description, attendee list, and any attached documents automatically. If you also have Google Drive connected, it can read linked documents and incorporate their content.

The morning briefing

The best time to run this prompt is every morning:

```
Good morning. Please check my calendar for today and give me:
1. A summary of all meetings today with times
2. A pre-meeting brief for each one
3. Any conflicts or back-to-back meetings I should be aware of
4. Blocks of free time I could use for deep work

If any meetings have Google Drive documents attached, read them, and include key
points in the relevant brief.
```

This single prompt, run at 8:30 AM, replaces 15–20 minutes of manual calendar review and preparation. Some readers save this as a morning routine they run every workday.

During the meeting: Transcription

Transcription still runs as a separate service. Otter.ai, Fireflies.ai, or your video platform's built-in transcription captures the conversation. Your job during the meeting: give it your full attention.

Tool	Strengths	Integration note
Otter.ai	Real-time transcription, speaker ID, auto-joins Zoom/Meet	Transcripts exportable to Claude/ChatGPT or accessed via API
Fireflies.ai	Auto-join, AI summaries, topic tracking, CRM integrations	Built-in integrations with Slack, Notion, and Asana for auto distribution
Built-in (Zoom/Meet/Teams)	No additional tool needed, included with platform	Transcripts are downloadable. Zoom AI Companion and Teams Copilot generate summaries natively.

Table 4.1 - Transcription options. Start with your platform's built-in option. Add a dedicated tool for better accuracy or richer integrations

Note

Inform participants

Most jurisdictions and professional norms require that you inform meeting participants when a call is being recorded or transcribed. Your transcription tool will typically announce itself. If not, mention it at the start.

After the meeting: The connected packet workflow

This is where connected AI transforms the experience. Instead of exporting, pasting, and copying, the AI reads the transcript, generates the packet, and pushes action items to your task tool — all in one conversation.

The extraction and distribution process

You should try out the following prompt with one of your meeting transcripts. Replace the square brackets with the transcript:

```
I just finished a meeting. Here is the transcript.
Please produce a structured meeting packet:

1. DECISIONS MADE
   Write each decision as a clear sentence with who decided.

2. ACTION ITEMS
   For each: task, owner, deadline (TBD if not stated), one sentence of context.

3. OPEN QUESTIONS
   What was raised but not resolved?

4. EXECUTIVE SUMMARY
   3-5 sentences for someone who was not there.

After generating the packet, please:
- Send the summary and action items to the attendees via Gmail
- Create tasks in [Asana/Linear/Notion] for each action item with the assigned
owner and deadline
- Save this packet to my Meeting Packets folder in Google Drive

TRANSCRIPT:
[paste or upload the transcript file]
```

With Gmail, a task tool, and Drive connected, the AI generates the packet, distributes it, creates tasks, and archives the record. The AI shows you the draft email and proposed tasks for approval, but the manual steps of copying, formatting, and ticket creation are gone.

The review step

Even with connected tools, you remain the quality gate. Before approving, check for the following:

- **Are the action items correctly assigned?** The AI sometimes misattributes ownership. Fix before it creates tasks in the wrong person's queue.
- **Are decisions accurately captured?** Implicit decisions won't appear. Add them manually.

- **Is there anything sensitive?** Redact confidential content before distribution.
- **Is the summary accurate?** Read as if you were not in the meeting.

Once approved, the AI drafts the email, creates the tasks, and saves the packet. Post-meeting takes 5–7 minutes of review instead of 20–30 minutes of manual work.

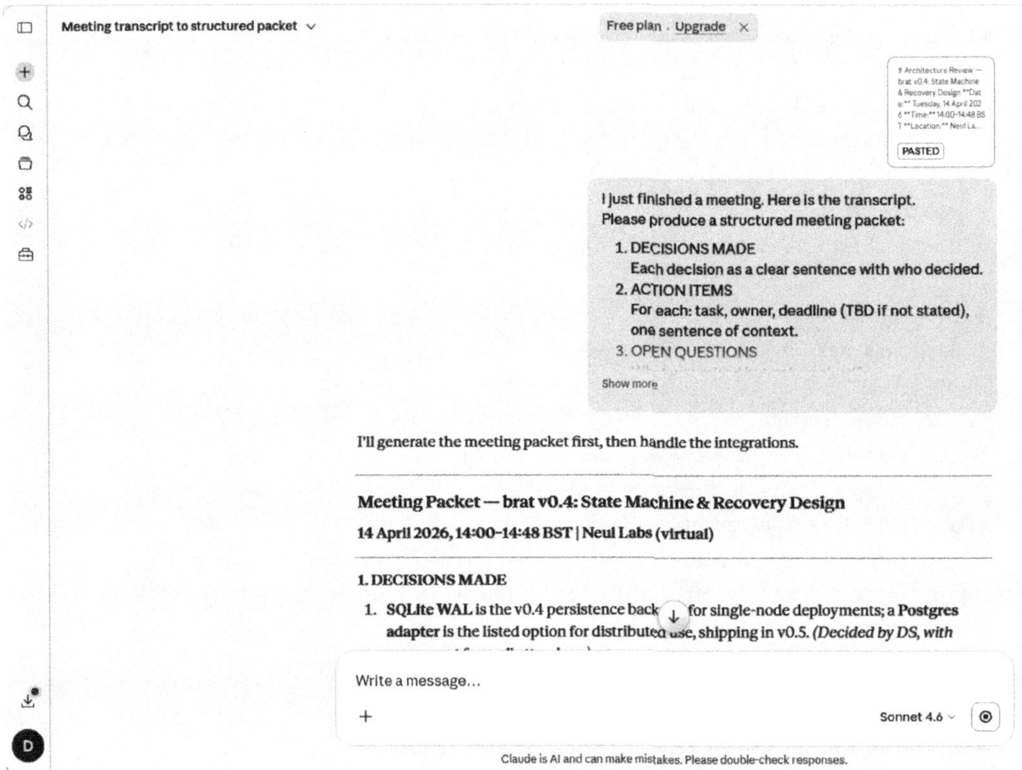

Figure 4.2 – The post meeting prompt in action

In the following example, the the AI extracts action items from the transcript provided. It also marks the owners and deadlines for your convenience.

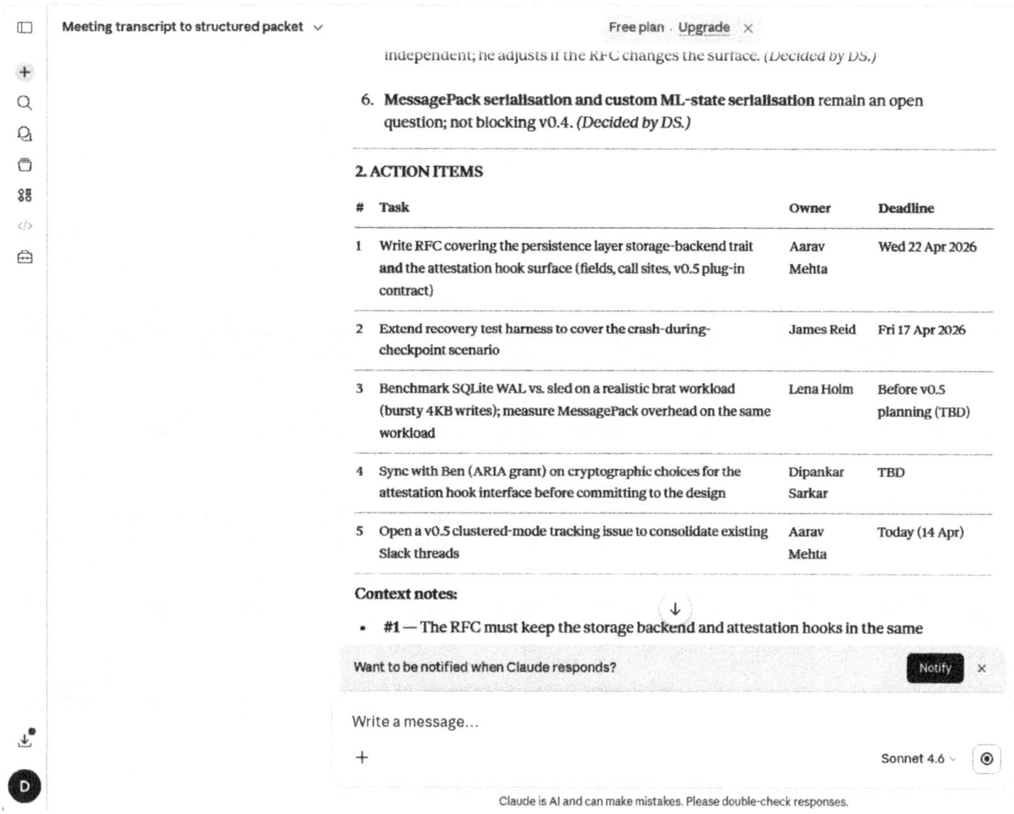

Figure 4.3 – Some sample generated action items

In the following example, the AI is requesting me to connect to Asana, Linear, or similar task-tracking tools to update the follow-up tasks from the meeting. If the AI had access to the email addresses of the participants, it would have drafted an email, ready to be edited and sent out.

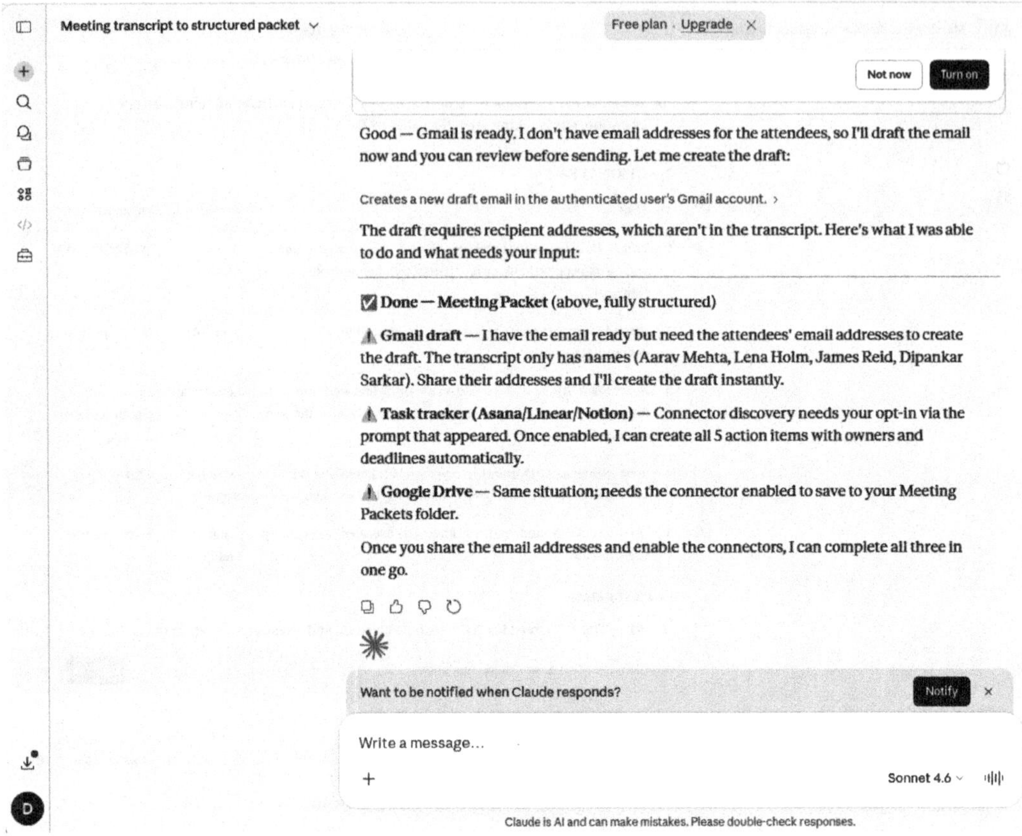

Figure 4.4 – Claude asking for additional data sources

Try this out and you will spend far less time working through multiple tabs of various systems at your workplace.

Recurring meetings: The feedback loop

Recurring meetings benefit the most from connected automation because each meeting's output feeds the next meeting's preparation automatically. Use the following prompt:

```
I have a recurring [weekly/biweekly] meeting with [group] coming up. Please:

1. Check my calendar for the meeting details
2. Search my Google Drive for the most recent meeting packet from this group
3. Check [Asana/Linear] for any open action items from previous meetings with this
group
```

```
Then generate a pre-meeting brief:
- FOLLOW-UPS: Which action items are due or overdue?
- CARRYOVER: Open questions from last time
- NEW TOPICS: Based on calendar context
- SUGGESTED AGENDA: 3-5 items based on all the above
```

The AI reads your calendar for context, searches Drive for the last packet, and checks your task tool for open items without you finding, opening, or pasting anything. Over time, this creates institutional memory for every recurring meeting.

> **Tip**
>
> **Save packets to a shared folder**
>
> Ask the AI to save each meeting packet to a specific Google Drive folder. Over time, this builds a searchable archive. When someone asks, "When did we decide to change the timeline?" you can search the folder and find the answer in seconds.

Advanced: Cross-meeting synthesis

For project leads sitting in multiple meetings, connected AI enables a powerful synthesis:

```
Search my Google Drive for all meeting packets from the past two weeks related to
[project name]. Then produce a synthesis:

1. PROGRESS SUMMARY across all meetings
2. OUTSTANDING ACTIONS: consolidated, deduplicated
3. DECISIONS LOG: chronological order
4. RISKS: flagged across any meeting
5. RECOMMENDED FOCUS for this week
```

This takes information scattered across five separate packets and condenses it into a single project-level view. This is extraordinarily useful for status reports (*Chapter 6*) and stakeholder updates.

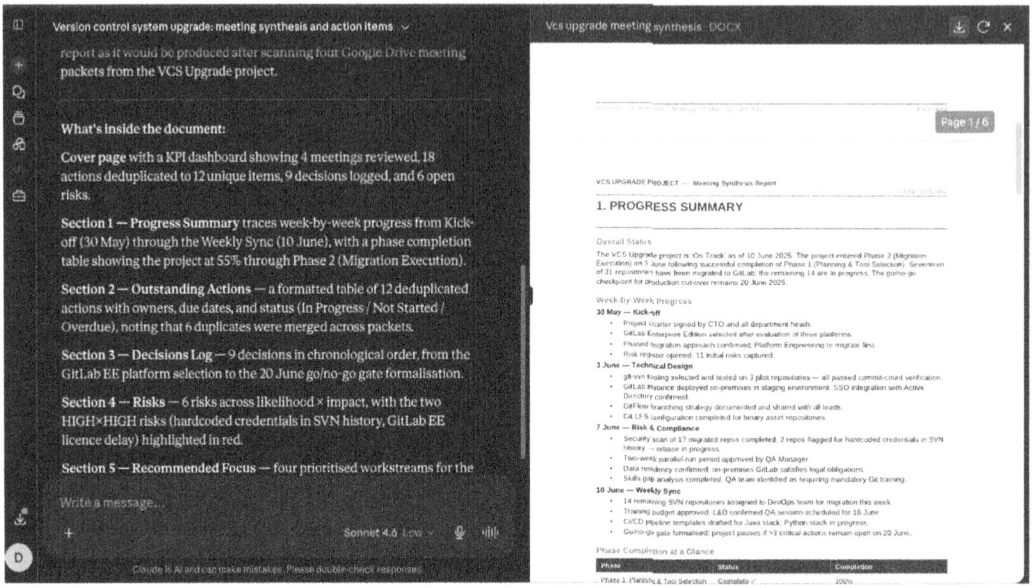

Figure 4.5 – Full report document created by Claude based on meetings

Fallback: When connections are unavailable

Not every workplace allows external AI integrations. If you cannot connect your tools, the workflows still work with a manual copy-paste step:

- **Pre-meeting briefs:** Copy calendar event details and paste into the AI manually
- **Transcript processing:** Export transcript as text and upload to the AI
- **Action item tracking:** Copy action items from AI output and create tasks manually

The time savings are smaller without connections (an extra 3–5 minutes per meeting on copy-paste), but the core prompts are identical. Start manual if you need to, and add connections when your organization permits.

Summary

In this chapter you have achieved the following for your meeting workflows:

- **Before**: AI reads your calendar and generates briefs automatically. A single morning prompt prepares you for every meeting of the day.
- **During**: Transcription runs in the background so that you can pay full attention to the conversation.

- **After**: AI generates a packet, generates email draft for Gmail, creates tasks in your tracker, and saves to Drive — all in one step.
- **Recurring**: Feedback loop where AI pulls the last packet and checks open tasks to prepare the next brief.
- **Synthesis**: AI pulls multiple packets from Drive and consolidates into a project-level view.

At six meetings per day, the overhead drops from 3+ hours to under an hour. More importantly, action items push directly to tools where they are tracked, and every meeting builds a searchable archive.

We now apply the same connected model to research in *Chapter 5* — using AI that searches the web and reads your documents to produce sourced briefs without tab-hopping.

Get this book's PDF version and more

Scan the QR code (or go to `packtpub.com/unlock`). Search for this book by name, confirm the edition, and then follow the steps on the page.

UNLOCK NOW

Note: Keep your invoice handy. Purchases made directly from Packt don't require an invoice.

5

Research in 30 Minutes, Not 3 Hours

Professional research in 2026 typically looks like this: open Google, type a query, open ten tabs, skim three, get distracted by a tangent, open five more, lose track of what you have read, copy snippets into a document, and eventually assemble something that feels incomplete but good enough because you have already spent two hours.

Finding information is not difficult. The challenge is to synthesize it across multiple sources into something coherent. You are simultaneously searching, reading, and organizing. Connected AI handles two of those three, leaving you to focus on evaluating whether the synthesis is accurate and useful.

This chapter builds on the connected model from *Chapter 4*. Instead of manually gathering sources and pasting them into AI, you will use tools that search the web natively, read your existing documents from Google Drive, and combine external research with internal context in a single conversation.

What you will achieve: You will use AI that searches the web, reads your existing documents, and synthesizes both into sourced briefs without opening a browser tab or copy-pasting a single URL.

The connected research stack

Research uses three capabilities, and all of these are available without leaving your AI tool:

Capability	What it does	Available in
Web search	AI searches the live web and returns results with source citations. No tab-hopping is required.	Claude (built-in web search), ChatGPT (browsing), Perplexity (purpose-built)
Document reading	AI reads files from your Google Drive, uploaded documents, or linked URLs to incorporate internal context.	Claude (Google Drive integration), ChatGPT (file upload, Drive plugins)
Deep research	AI conducts extended, multi-step research autonomously, searching, reading, cross-referencing, and synthesizing for several minutes.	Claude (deep research mode), ChatGPT (deep research), Perplexity Pro

Table 5.1 - The connected research stack

The key insight: when AI can both search the web and read your documents, it can produce research that combines external facts with your specific context. "How does our competitor's pricing compare to our current model?" requires both web data and internal documents. Connected AI handles this in one prompt.

The four-step research workflow

The goal of this workflow is to enable you to do deep research without navigating search engines, ads, and misinformation, and get high quality outputs.

Step 1: Define the question

A vague question produces a vague brief. Write down the specific question in one sentence before opening any tool.

Bad: `What's happening in AI?`

Good: `What are the three leading AI transcription services for enterprise teams with GDPR requirements, and how do they compare on price, accuracy, and integration?`

A well-defined question has three properties: a specific topic, a clear scope, and an implied output format.

> Tip
>
> **The "would one Google search answer this?" test**
>
> If a single search would give you the answer, use regular search. This workflow is for questions requiring synthesis across multiple sources, comparison of options, or structured analysis.

Step 2: Gather and synthesize

This is where connected AI replaces the tab-hopping. You have three approaches depending on what the research requires.

Approach A: Web search for current facts

When you need up-to-date information from the public web, market data, competitor moves, or recent developments, use your AI tool's built-in web search:

```
Search the web and answer: what are the current best practices for onboarding AI
tools in teams of 10-50 people? I need: typical timelines, common failure modes,
and what a good rollout plan looks like. Cite your sources for each claim.
```

Claude, ChatGPT, and Perplexity all search the web and return answers with source citations. Without you having to open a browser, the AI does the searching, reading, and initial synthesis.

Approach B: Internal documents for company context

When the research requires your company's internal data, past decisions, existing strategies, or internal metrics, use the Drive integration:

```
Search my Google Drive for documents related to our AI adoption strategy. Read the
most recent strategy document and our Q4 implementation report. Then summarize
what we have already decided, what is in progress, and what gaps remain.
```

The AI will look into all your cloud files to build an understanding of what has been going on within your private and organizational context.

Approach C: Combined external + internal

The most powerful research combines both. With the following prompt, the AI searches the web for external context and reads your Drive for internal context:

```
I need to assess whether we should switch from [current tool] to [competitor].

Please:
1. Search the web for recent reviews, pricing, and feature comparisons of
[competitor]
2. Read our existing vendor evaluation document in Google Drive (search for
"vendor evaluation")
3. Produce a comparison that maps the competitor's features against our current
requirements

Format as a structured brief with a recommendation.
```

In the following image, you can see how the AI has both public and private data sources to give you a research output that can be used to augment decision-making.

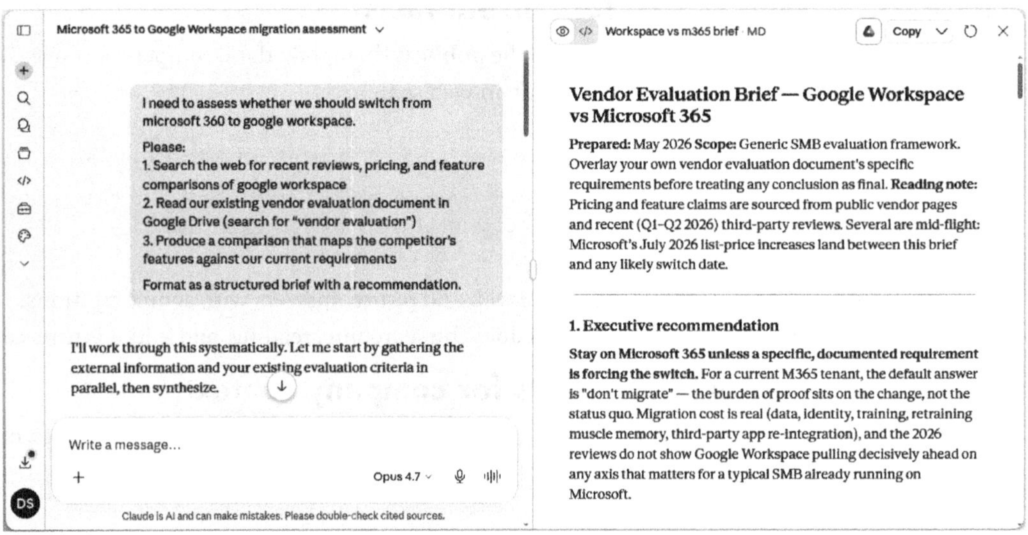

Figure 5.1 – A full research output from Claude

Approach D: Deep research for complex questions

For questions requiring extensive investigation, use the deep research feature available in Claude and ChatGPT. Deep research conducts an autonomous, multi-step investigation over several minutes, searching multiple sources, cross-referencing findings, and producing a comprehensive report. Use this prompt:

```
Use deep research to investigate: what is the current regulatory landscape for AI
in financial services across the UK, EU, and US? I need: key regulations in
effect, pending legislation, enforcement trends, and practical implications for a
fintech company deploying AI for compliance workflows.

Produce a structured brief with confidence levels for each finding and full source
citations.
```

Deep research takes 3–5 minutes to run but replaces what would be 3–5 hours of manual research. The output is typically a comprehensive report with dozens of sources, structured findings, and confidence levels/ratings. Use it for high-stakes research tasks where thoroughness matters more than speed.

The confidence level per finding is the most important addition. It forces the AI to distinguish between claims backed by multiple quality sources and claims from a single blog post. This is the difference between research you can act on and research that might mislead you.

> Note
>
> **When to use deep research vs. standard search**
>
> Standard web search is for focused questions with clear answers (pricing, feature comparisons, latest news). Deep research is for complex, multi-faceted questions that require synthesizing across many sources (regulatory landscapes, market analyses, technology evaluations). If your question would require opening 20+ tabs manually, use deep research.

Step 3: Structure the brief

Raw research output is not
a deliverable. You should also review the output at a high level to ensure there are no obvious issues like topical or information hallucinations. The following prompt will then help you shape it into a format useful for its audience:

```
Structure this research as a brief with:

RESEARCH BRIEF: [topic]
Date: [today] | Prepared for: [audience]
```

```
EXECUTIVE SUMMARY
3-5 sentences. Lead with the conclusion.

KEY FINDINGS
For each finding:
- The finding (one clear sentence)
- Supporting evidence (with sources)
- Confidence: HIGH / MEDIUM / LOW

COMPARISON TABLE (if applicable)

GAPS AND LIMITATIONS
What could not be determined?

SOURCES
Numbered list with URLs.
```

Step 4: Verify

AI research tools can hallucinate false claims and present them with confidence, invent sources, and misrepresent findings. Verification is not optional. Use the following checklist to validate the output:

1. **Check sources exist.** Click 3–5 cited URLs. Do the pages exist?
2. **Check sources match claims.** For key findings, confirm the source says what the brief claims
3. **Check recency.** Are sources current enough for your purpose?
4. **Check for missing perspectives.** Does the brief present only one side of a genuine debate?
5. **Check numbers.** Verify headline statistics against primary sources. Numerical hallucination is common.

> Tip
>
> **How much verification?**
>
> Depends on stakes. Internal exploration: spot-check 3–5 sources. Board presentation or client deliverable: verify every key claim and every number. Verification adds 10–20 minutes, but it is still dramatically faster than manual research.

Five research patterns

We will now start looking at what research patterns expert AI users are using. Most professional research falls into five patterns. Each prompt is designed for connected AI; it may search the web, read your Drive, or both.

Pattern 1: Competitive landscape

The following prompt will help you assess the competitive landscape:

```
Search the web for the competitive landscape of [market]. Also check my Google
Drive for any existing competitor analyses.

For each major player: positioning, key product, target customer, pricing,
strengths, weaknesses.
Include emerging players from the past 12 months.
Format as a comparison table plus summary.
```

Pattern 2: Decision support

The following prompt will help you build the case for a given decision:

```
I need to decide between [Option A, B, C] for [purpose].
My criteria: [1] cost, [2] integration, [3] adoption.

Search the web for current information on each option. If I have evaluations in
Google Drive, read those too.
Evaluate each option against all criteria with evidence. Recommend with reasoning.
Flag where it is close.
```

Pattern 3: Trend analysis

This prompt will help you identify key trends in your professional domain:

```
What are the key trends in [domain] over the past [timeframe]? For each trend:
- What is happening and why
- Who is driving it
- Evidence (data, reports, examples)
- What it means for [my industry/company]

Distinguish strong-evidence trends from speculative. I need to present this to
[audience] and cannot cite hype as fact.
```

> **Tip**
>
> **Combine patterns**
>
> Real research often combines patterns. A competitive landscape might include trend analysis. A decision brief might open with a state-of-the-art overview. Use patterns as building blocks.

This section gave you new ideas on how to do research in your own work. We will now discuss how to ensure you produce validated, high-quality documents.

Handling hallucinations

Hallucination is the biggest risk in AI research. It is also manageable if you know where to look.

Here's where hallucinations are most common:

- **Statistics and numbers.** AI frequently generates plausible-sounding statistics with no actual source
- **Source citations.** AI can generate URLs that look real but lead nowhere
- **Recency claims.** Outdated information might be presented as current
- **Nuance.** "Preliminary evidence suggests" becomes "research shows" in the AI's output

Prompting for honesty

Always use this to check the output you might want to share or publish:

```
Important guidelines for this research:
- Only include claims you can cite to a specific source
- If uncertain, say so explicitly
- Distinguish "well-established" from "preliminary"
- If a statistic lacks a verifiable source, omit it
- Flag areas where sources disagree
```

You can include this prompt at the start of your interaction, but in practice, it works best at the end, once you've spent enough time exploring the topic with the AI. At that point, it's worth thinking about how to share your research with other stakeholders across different contexts.

From research to action

Connected AI makes the handoff from research to action seamless. The research you've just done isn't a static document — it's working context the AI can immediately reuse. The same brief can become any of the following:

- **Research → report:** Tell the AI to use the brief as input for a document generation chain. No copy-paste needed since the research is already in the conversation.
- **Research → presentation:** The executive summary and comparison tables map directly to slides.
- **Research → meeting brief:** Save the brief to Drive and the AI can pull it into a pre-meeting packet automatically.
- **Research → email:** Ask the AI to draft an email summarizing the research for a colleague. With Gmail connected, it can create the draft for your approval.

When both research and downstream outputs are AI-assisted and connected, the time from "I need to understand X" to "here is a polished deliverable about X" drops from days to hours.

> Tip
>
> **Save research briefs to Drive**
>
> Ask the AI to save every research brief to a specific Drive folder: `Save this brief as a Google Doc titled 'Research [topic] [date]' in my Research folder.` This builds a searchable knowledge base. Future prompts can reference past research: `Check my Research folder for anything related to [topic] before starting.`

Summary

In this chapter, you have achieved the following:

- **Implemented four research approaches**, including web search for external facts, Drive reading for internal context, combined for both, and deep research for complex investigations
- **Tried three research patterns** (competitive landscape, decision support, trend analysis) with connected prompts

- **Used a verification checklist** and prompting techniques for reducing hallucination
- **Achieved seamless handoff** from research to reports, presentations, emails, and meeting briefs through connected tools

The time shift: 30–45 minutes including verification replaces 2–3 hours. The quality shift: structured briefs with sources and confidence levels, plus internal context that manual research rarely incorporates.

The next chapter will turn raw inputs including research briefs, meeting packets, and Drive documents into polished first drafts using connected document generation chains.

Get this book's PDF version and more

Scan the QR code (or go to `packtpub.com/unlock`). Search for this book by name, confirm the edition, and then follow the steps on the page.

UNLOCK NOW

Note: Keep your invoice handy. Purchases made directly from Packt don't require an invoice.

6

First Drafts in 15 Minutes

The hardest part of writing any document is the first ten minutes. You stare at the blank page. You write an opening, delete it, write another, and delete that. You check your email. You come back, reread, and start a third time.

AI eliminated the blank page in *Chapter 2*. But in that chapter, you still had to gather your inputs manually and copy the output into its destination. This chapter eliminates those steps too. The AI reads your inputs from connected sources—meeting packets from Drive, research briefs from the same conversation, task data from your project tool—and writes the finished document directly to where it needs to go.

Your role shifts decisively from writer to editor, and the editing happens faster because the AI already has all the context.

Note

Before you begin

The workflows in this chapter assume the AI has live, authenticated access to your Drive, mail, and task tools. That access is not yet a universal default. Whether you can reproduce a given chain end-to-end depends on your AI platform, the connectors it supports, your organization's IT and data policies, and in some cases the tier of your subscription. A workflow that runs cleanly on one stack may require a paid plan, an enterprise admin's approval, or simply not exist as an option on another.

Rather than treating each chain as a recipe to copy exactly, treat it as a pattern. The four-step structure — extract, structure, draft, and deliver — holds regardless of which specific tools you have wired up. If Drive is not connected but SharePoint is, the prompt changes by one word. If no task tool is connected at all, that step becomes a manual paste and the rest of the chain still works. Where a chain depends on a specific integration to function, we will flag it; everywhere else, substitute what you have.

What you will achieve: You will build document generation chains where AI pulls inputs from your Drive, meeting packets, and research briefs, drafts the document, and saves the finished output back to Drive or creates the draft on Gmail, all without leaving the conversation.

The connected document generation chain

The chain has four steps, same as before, but now the AI gathers inputs and delivers outputs through connected tools:

Step	Action	Your role	Connected tools used
1	AI gathers input from connected sources	Verify nothing is missed	Google Drive, email, task tool
2	AI proposes an outline	Approve, rearrange, or redirect	None (conversation only)
3	AI drafts each section	Review for accuracy	None (conversation only)

Step	Action	Your role	Connected tools used
4	AI polishes and delivers	Final review, approve send	Google Drive, Gmail

Table 6.1 - The connected document generation chain. Steps 1 and 4 use integrations to gather inputs and deliver outputs. Steps 2 and 3 happen in conversation

Let's explore these steps in detail.

Step 1: Connected extraction

This activity benefits most from the approach in *Chapter 4*, where we worked with transcripts to generate meeting packets. Instead of manually gathering and pasting inputs, tell the AI where to find them:

```
I need to write a [weekly status report / proposal / client summary]. Please
gather the inputs:

1. Search my Google Drive for meeting packets from this week related to [project]
2. Check [Asana/Linear] for completed and in-progress tasks this week
3. Read the email thread with [person] about [topic] from my Gmail

Extract and organize the key content for this document. Flag any gaps where I may
need to add information.

Audience: [who reads this]
Purpose: [what they should know or do after reading]
Length: [target]
```

The AI searches your Drive, checks your task tool, and reads relevant emails, all without you opening any of those applications. It returns an organized extraction with gaps flagged. You verify that the extraction is complete, add anything missing, and move to *Step 2*.

> Note
>
> **The "do not invent" rule still applies**
>
> Connected extraction does not change the fundamental rule: the AI should never add facts that are not in the inputs. Add this to every chain: `Only include content from the sources you read. If a section has insufficient content, mark it as [NEEDS INPUT] rather than producing filler content.`

Step 2: Outline

To generate an outline, use the following prompt:

```
Based on the extracted content, propose an outline.
For each section:
- Heading
- What it covers (1-2 sentences)
- Which source content feeds into it

Optimize for the audience: they care most about [key priorities, e.g., "the bottom
line and next steps" or "technical details and risk assessment"].
```

Review the outline before proceeding. Rearranging the outline stage takes 30 seconds. After the full draft is written, it takes 10 minutes to review it. If the structure is wrong, redirect it now.

> Tip
>
> **Reuse outlines for recurring documents**
>
> If you write the same type of document weekly, save the outline as a Google Doc in your Drive. In future chains, tell the AI: `Read the status report template from my Drive and use that structure.` This way, you can skip *Step 2* entirely.

Step 3: Draft

Input this prompt to create the draft:

```
Using the approved outline, write the full draft.

Guidelines:
- Write in a [professional / conversational] tone
- Keep total length to [target]
- Use only content from the extracted sources
- Mark gaps as [NEEDS INPUT], never fill with filler
- Lead each section with the key takeaway

Refer to my custom instructions for voice and style.
```

Review for accuracy first. Did the AI add anything not present in your inputs? Did it misrepresent a number or timeline? Did it fill a gap with confident-sounding language?

Accuracy errors are the highest risk because they look professional and travel downstream undetected.

Step 4: Polish and deliver

This is where connected AI shines. After the polish pass, the AI delivers the document to its destination:

```
Review and polish this draft:
1. Tighten language and cut 10-15% without losing content
2. Strengthen the opening with the key takeaway
3. Ensure smooth transitions between sections
4. Clear call to action in the closing

Then:
- Save the final version as a Google Doc titled "[Document name] [date]" in my
[folder] on Drive
- Email it to [recipients] via Gmail with subject: "[subject line]" and a brief
cover note summarizing the key points
```

The AI produces the polished draft, shows you the final version and the draft email for approval, then saves and drafts. The entire chain from gathering inputs to a delivered document happens in a single conversation.

The four-step pattern — extraction, structuring, drafting, and polish and delivery — works for almost any recurring document you produce. What changes between document types is the mix of sources and the shape of the output. The next section walks through three of the most common chains in detail, so you can adapt the templates directly to your own work.

Three connected document chains

The chains below cover documents most knowledge workers produce on a regular cadence: a weekly status report, a project proposal, and a client-facing summary. Each one shows the connected tools involved, the prompts that drive each step, and the points where you should expect to intervene. Treat them as starting templates rather than fixed recipes. Once the pattern is familiar, mixing and matching steps across chains becomes second nature.

Chain 1: Weekly status report

This is the most common recurring document. With connected tools, the entire input gathering phase is automated. You can also add tools not shown here, such as SharePoint or

Dropbox, for example, depending on where your team's information lives. Use this prompt to create your weekly status report and replace the squared brackets with your own input:

```
It is Friday. I need to write my weekly status report.

Please:
1. Search my Google Drive for all meeting packets from this week
2. Check [Asana/Linear] for tasks completed, in progress, and blocked this week
3. Read any emails I sent to [manager] this week for additional context

Then produce a status report with:
- Overall status (one sentence: on track / at risk)
- Key accomplishments
- In progress
- Blockers and risks
- Next week's priorities

Keep it under 400 words. Save to my Status Reports folder in Drive and email to
[manager].
```

From a single prompt, the AI gathers a full week of context from three sources, drafts the report, saves it, and emails it. Time: 5–10 minutes of review. Compare this to the 60–90 minutes of manually gathering and writing the same report typically required.

Chain 2: Project proposal

Proposals are higher-stakes and draw on both research and internal context. Use this prompt to create your project proposals:

```
I need to write a proposal for [initiative].

Please gather:
1. The research brief I saved to Drive on [topic] (search my Research folder)
2. Any related meeting packets from the past month
3. Our current budget document (search Drive for "[budget doc name]")

Then produce a proposal:
- Executive summary (the ask and the why)
- Problem statement
- Proposed solution
- Expected outcomes with metrics
- Costs and timeline
```

```
- Risks and mitigations
- Next steps

Audience: [who approves this].
Keep it to 2-3 pages. Lead with the recommendation, not the problem.
```

> **Tip**
>
> **Feed prior proposals as style templates**
>
> Ask the AI to read a successful past proposal from Drive: `Also read 'Q3 Proposal Data Platform' from my Drive and match that tone and structure level.` The AI uses it as a style reference without you extracting and pasting examples.

Chain 3: Client-facing summary

Client documents carry the additional constraint of representing your company. Connected tools ensure nothing is missing from the meeting record. Use this prompt to prepare your client-facing summaries:

```
I need to write a client summary for [client] following our meeting on [date].

Please:
1. Find the meeting packet from that date in Drive
2. Read the email thread with [client] from the past week in Gmail for additional
context
3. Check [Asana] for deliverables due for this client

Produce a summary:
- What was discussed or delivered
- Key outcomes or findings
- Next steps with owners and dates
- Open items

Tone: professional, warm. Do NOT include internal commentary or information the
client should not see.

Save to my Client folder in Drive and draft an email to [client contact] via Gmail
for my review.
```

Note

Client-facing safety check

Before approving any AI-generated client document: (1) check for internal language the client should not see, (2) verify all commitments and timelines, (3) ensure tone matches your actual client relationship. AI defaults to generic professional tone; adjust for the specific relationship.

Even with the safety check in place, connected document chains do not always run cleanly end-to-end. Failures tend to cluster in a handful of predictable patterns, and recognizing them early is what separates a useful chain from one that produces flawed output. The next section walks through the most common failures and how to recover from them.

When the chain goes wrong

The following failure modes cover the majority of what you will encounter in practice. Each has a distinct signature, and each is fixable without restarting the chain—provided you catch it at the right step. The rule of thumb: fix structural problems by redirecting earlier in the chain, and fix surface problems (tone, length, phrasing) with targeted follow-ups on the draft.

The AI invents content

Despite the "do not invent" instruction, the AI occasionally fills gaps. This is most common with numbers, dates, and names. Fix: check every fact in the draft against the extraction output. If a claim was not in the extraction, delete it or verify it independently.

The structure does not fit

If the outline feels wrong, do not proceed hoping the draft will fix it. Redirect at *Step 2*. The most common problem: leading with background when the audience wants the recommendation first.

The tone is wrong

Use a targeted follow-up:

```
The tone needs adjustment:
- Section 1: more formal for this audience
- Closing: make it a more confident and clear recommendation, not a tentative suggestion
- Throughout: remove hedging like "perhaps" and "it might be worth considering"
```

The document is too long

You can keep following up until it works to your exact requirements:

```
This draft is [X words]. Cut to [Y words].
Keep: the executive summary, recommendation, and data.
Cut: background context, repetitive points, anything repeating content covered
elsewhere.
```

Building your connected template library

After using the chain for a few document types, your prompts stabilize. Your weekly status report uses the same chain every Friday. Your client summaries follow the same structure with different content.

Save your proven chains as Google Docs in a `Templates` folder on Drive. Each template includes:

- **Document type and audience.** Example: `Weekly status report for the leadership team`
- **Connected sources.** Which Drive folders, task projects, and email threads to check
- **The four-step chain.** The exact prompts, refined from experience
- **Known issues.** Recurring problems with this document type: The AI tends to understate risks. Always review the risk section manually.

When you need to write the document, tell the AI: `Read my status report template from Drive and run the chain.` One prompt triggers the entire workflow.

> Tip
>
> **Share templates with your team**
>
> Save templates in a shared Drive folder. This way, everyone produces consistent, high-quality documents and new team members start producing useful output on day one by running a template chain.

The editor mindset

This chapter deepens the mental shift from *Chapter 2*. With connected inputs and outputs, the AI handles gathering, structuring, drafting, formatting, and distributing. You handle four things:

- **Accuracy**. Every fact is traceable to inputs. Anything else is wrong.
- **Completeness**. Nothing important is missing. Gaps flagged and filled.
- **Structure**. Logical flow. Key message up front.
- **Voice**. Sounds like you. Appropriate for the audience.

If all four pass, the document is done. If any fail, steer with a follow-up prompt. This *evaluate-steer loop* is faster than writing from scratch and produces more consistent results because your prompts improve with every use.

Summary

In this chapter, you accomplished the following:

- **Made a connected four-step chain** where AI gathers inputs from Drive, email, and task tools, drafts the document, and delivers it to Drive and Gmail
- **Tried three complete chains** for weekly status reports, project proposals, and client summaries each using connected inputs
- **Adopted the editor mindset** where you evaluated AI output for accuracy, completeness, structure, and voice

The time shift: a document that took 2–4 hours now takes 15–30 minutes of prompting and reviewing. But the real shift is that gathering inputs, writing, formatting, and distributing are no longer separate tasks that fragment your day. They are a single conversation that produces a delivered result.

In the next chapter we will tackle coordination, extracting tasks from meetings, messages, and email threads and pushing them directly to your project tracker.

Get this book's PDF version and more

Scan the QR code (or go to `packtpub.com/unlock`). Search for this book by name, confirm the edition, and then follow the steps on the page.

UNLOCK NOW

Note: Keep your invoice handy. Purchases made directly from Packt don't require an invoice.

7

Tracked Tasks in 15 Mins

Knowledge work generates tasks constantly. Every meeting produces action items. Every email thread spawns follow-ups. Every Slack conversation buries a "can you handle this by Friday?" somewhere in the middle of a thirty-message thread. The tasks are scattered across a dozen sources, expressed in natural language rather than structured formats, and it's nobody's job to collect them.

The result is the coordination tax: the time you spend not doing the work but tracking it. This may include reading through transcripts to find what was promised, scrolling through email to remember what you agreed to, or manually creating tickets in Asana or Linear for things that were decided in a meeting forty minutes ago. For most managers and team leads, this overhead consumes 30–60 minutes a day.

Connected AI eliminates this by reading the same sources you would—transcripts, emails, documents—extracting the tasks automatically, and pushing them directly to your project tracker. You review the extracted tasks, correct any misattributions, and approve. The manual step of creating tickets disappears.

What you will achieve: You will have AI reading your meeting transcripts, email threads, and Slack-style messages, extracting every task with an owner and deadline, and pushing them directly to your project tracker. This way, nothing falls through the cracks, and you never manually create a ticket from meeting notes again.

The connected task extraction stack

Before walking through the workflow itself, it helps to see the moving parts. A task extraction chain has three layers: the sources the AI reads from, the AI itself doing the extraction, and the destination where the structured tasks land. Each layer is swappable — the value comes from connecting them, not from any specific tool in any specific slot. The following table shows the most common combinations:

Layer	Sources	What the AI does
Input sources	Meeting packets in Drive, email threads in Gmail, uploaded transcripts, Slack exports	Reads unstructured conversations and documents to identify commitments, requests, and action items.
AI processor	Claude or ChatGPT with connectors	Extracts tasks with owner, deadline, context, and dependencies. Flags ambiguous items for your review.
Task destination	Asana, Linear, Notion, Jira, Google Tasks (via integration)	Creates tickets/tasks directly in your project tool with the extracted metadata.

Table 7.1 - The task extraction stack. AI reads unstructured sources, extracts structured tasks, and pushes them to your tracker

Note

Connecting your task tool

Claude and ChatGPT support integrations with major project management tools including Asana, Linear, Notion, and Jira. Once connected, the AI can create tasks, assign owners, set deadlines, and add context notes, all from within a conversation. Setup takes 5–10 minutes via the **Connectors** panel. See the *Appendix* for step-by-step instructions.

Extracting tasks from meetings

This is the highest-volume source of hidden tasks. You already generate meeting packets in *Chapter 4*. Task extraction extends that workflow: after the AI produces the packet, it pushes the action items directly to your project tool.

The integrated meeting-to-task prompt

Now with all the connected data sources, you can use the following prompt to integrate the complete workflow. Please replace the square brackets with your transcript:

```
Here is a transcript from a meeting that just ended.
Please:

1. Extract all action items. For each:
   - Task: what needs to be done (specific, actionable)
   - Owner: who is responsible (use names from transcript)
   - Deadline: date if mentioned, otherwise TBD
   - Context: one sentence of background
   - Priority: HIGH / MEDIUM / LOW based on discussion urgency

2. Flag any task where ownership is ambiguous as NEEDS CLARIFICATION

3. Create each task in [Asana/Linear/Notion] in the [project name] project,
assigned to the correct owner with the deadline set

4. Generate the standard meeting packet (decisions, open questions, summary) and
save to my Meeting Packets folder in Google Drive

TRANSCRIPT:
[paste or upload]
```

This prompt combines the *Chapter 4* meeting packet workflow with task creation. The AI reads the transcript, extracts the structured packet and the tasks simultaneously, creates the tasks in your project tool, and saves the packet to Drive.

Reviewing extracted tasks

The AI gets task extraction right about 85% of the time. The 15% where it needs your help:

- **Misattributed ownership:** The most common error. Someone says, "we should update the roadmap," and the AI guesses who "we" refers to. Fix before the task is created in the wrong person's queue.
- **Missed implicit tasks:** Sometimes a commitment is made through tone rather than explicit words. "I'll take a look" is a task that may not trigger extraction. Add these manually.
- **Over-extraction:** The AI may turn a casual suggestion into a formal task. "It might be worth checking the analytics" is not necessarily a task. Remove anything that was speculation, not commitment.
- **Missing deadlines**: If no deadline was stated, the AI marks TBD. You should set a reasonable deadline before creating the task, or it will sit untracked.

Extracting tasks from email threads

Email is where tasks go to hide. Someone requests something in paragraph three of a five-paragraph email. A follow-up gets buried in a thread. A commitment you made last Tuesday is sitting in your *Sent* folder with no corresponding ticket.

With Gmail connected (you can connect other email providers), the AI can scan your email for hidden tasks:

```
Search my Gmail for emails from the past [week / 3 days] where someone asked me to
do something, or where I committed to doing something. Extract all tasks:

- Task: what needs to be done
- Source: which email (sender, subject, date)
- Owner: me or someone else
- Deadline: if mentioned
- Status: not started / already done (check if I replied with the deliverable)

Present the list for my review before creating any tasks. Only create tasks in
[Asana/Linear] after I approve.
```

This is a weekly hygiene prompt. Run it every Friday afternoon or Monday morning to catch anything that slipped through the cracks during the week. The AI reads your email threads, identifies requests and commitments, and even checks whether you have already completed some of them. You review, remove false positives, and approve the remaining tasks for creation.

> **Tip**
>
> **Run this weekly, not daily**
>
> Daily extraction from email tends to produce false positives because many email requests resolve themselves within 24–48 hours. Weekly extraction catches the ones that did not resolve and creates tasks only for genuine open items.

Extracting tasks from documents and messages

Sometimes tasks hide in shared documents, Slack messages, or notes. For these, use a flexible extraction prompt. Please replace the square brackets with your transcript:

```
I have [a document / a set of messages / notes] that contain commitments and
action items. Please extract all tasks:

- Task: specific, actionable description
- Owner: who is responsible
- Deadline: if mentioned
- Context: where in the source this task was found

Source:
[paste the content, upload the file, or ask the AI to read it from Google Drive]
```

If your organization uses Slack, you can export conversations and upload them. Microsoft Teams works similarly: meeting transcripts and chat exports can be downloaded from the Teams admin or compliance interfaces and fed into the AI the same way, and where a Teams connector is available, the AI can read messages and transcripts directly. If the content lives in a Google Doc or a Word file on SharePoint or OneDrive, the AI reads it directly from the source. The extraction prompt is the same regardless of where the content comes from — the AI adapts to the format of the input.

The weekly status sweep

The most powerful task management workflow in this chapter is the weekly sweep: a single prompt that reviews your entire task portfolio and produces a status report:

```
Please review my task portfolio:

1. Check [Asana/Linear] for all tasks assigned to me or my team
```

```
2. Search my Google Drive for meeting packets from this week to catch any new
action items not yet in the tracker
3. Search my Gmail for any commitments I made this week that are not yet tracked

Then produce:
- OVERDUE: tasks past their deadline (flag these)
- DUE THIS WEEK: tasks due in the next 7 days
- NEW ITEMS: tasks from meetings and email not yet in the tracker (propose
creating these)
- COMPLETED: tasks I can mark as done based on evidence from email or Drive
- BLOCKED: anything that appears stalled

For new items, create tasks in [Asana/Linear] after my approval.
```

This sweep reads from three connected sources: your task tool, Drive, and Gmail, and reconciles them. It catches tasks that exist in email but not in the tracker, identifies tasks you completed but forgot to mark as done, and flags overdue items. In 10 minutes of review, you have a complete picture of everything on your plate.

> Note
>
> **Why this matters for teams**
>
> When everyone on a team runs the weekly sweep, the team's task tracker becomes the single source of truth. Tasks do not live in someone's memory or remain buried in an email thread. They are extracted, tracked, and visible. The coordination tax drops dramatically because the information is already where it needs to be.

From tasks to status summaries

Task data in your project tool is also an input for status reports (*Chapter 6*). With the task tool connected, you can generate summaries without manually compiling anything:

```
Read all tasks in the [Project Name] project in [Asana/Linear]. Generate a status
summary:

- Overall status: on track / at risk / blocked
- Completed this week: [count] tasks
- In progress: [count] tasks with owners
- Overdue: [count] tasks (list them specifically)
- Key risks or blockers
```

```
- Recommended priorities for next week

Keep it under 300 words. Format for [audience].
```

This is the handoff from *Chapter 7* to *Chapter 6*: task data becomes report input. The AI reads the live state of your project and produces a summary you can send directly or feed into a document generation chain, without any spreadsheet compilation or manual counting.

Handling ambiguity: When tasks are unclear

Real conversations produce ambiguous commitments. "Let's circle back on that"—is that a task? "I'll think about it"—is that a deliverable? The AI cannot resolve ambiguity that exists in the source material. What it can do is flag it.

The `NEEDS CLARIFICATION` flag in the extraction prompt is your tool for this. When the AI encounters an ambiguous commitment, it extracts the item but marks it for your attention:

```
NEEDS CLARIFICATION:
"David mentioned he would look into the vendor pricing."  Is this a formal task
with a deadline, or an informal intent? If it is a task, who should it be assigned
to and by when?
```

You resolve the ambiguity with a one-line response: `Yes, assign it to David, due next Friday`, and the AI creates the task. This is faster and more reliable than trying to catch these ambiguous commitments from memory a week later.

Fallback: Manual task extraction

If you cannot connect a task tool, the extraction workflow still works. The AI produces a structured task list in the conversation or as a document:

```
Extract tasks from this transcript. Format each as:

    Task description
    Owner: [name]
    Deadline: [date or TBD]
    Context: [one sentence]

I will create these in my project tool manually.
```

You then copy the list and create tasks by hand. The extraction still saves considerable time: the AI does the reading and structuring; you do the data entry. It is not as seamless as the connected version, but it is far better than reading through transcripts yourself.

Summary

In this chapter we have learned how to -

- **Extract tasks from meetings and emails:** AI reads transcripts, extracts tasks with owners and deadlines, and creates them in your project tool. This combines with the *Chapter 4* meeting packet workflow.
- **Do a weekly status sweep:** A single prompt that reads your task tool, Drive, and Gmail to reconcile your entire portfolio, catch untracked items, and flag overdue work.

When these chains work well, the time spent tracking rather than doing tends to shrink; for many people, a meaningful chunk of the day moves from manual reconciliation to a shorter review of AI-extracted tasks. Just as useful, fewer commitments slip through unnoticed, because items mentioned in a meeting, email, or message are more likely to be captured and assigned somewhere visible. How much of this you see in practice depends on which tools are connected and how disciplined your team is about writing things down.

In the next chapter, we tackle data: using AI to clean, analyze, and visualize spreadsheets without writing a single formula.

Get this book's PDF version and more

Scan the QR code (or go to `packtpub.com/unlock`). Search for this book by name, confirm the edition, and then follow the steps on the page.

UNLOCK NOW

Note: Keep your invoice handy. Purchases made directly from Packt don't require an invoice.

8

Spreadsheets Without Writing Formulas

You are not bad at spreadsheets. You are a professional who should not be spending two hours wrestling with XLOOKUP formulas, broken pivot tables, and color-coded conditional formatting when your actual job is making decisions from the data, rather than wrangling it into shape.

The traditional spreadsheet workflow is this: download CSV, open in Excel or Sheets, spot errors manually, write formulas, debug formulas, build pivot tables, format the output, copy it into a presentation or email, and explain what it means. AI compresses this into a conversation: describe what you need, the AI writes and runs the code, and you review the output.

This chapter is different from the previous ones in an important way. Instead of AI processing text (emails, transcripts, documents), it is processing data – running actual Python code internally on its servers to clean, transform, analyze, and visualize your numbers. You do not need to understand the Python code. You describe the outcome you want in plain English, and the AI handles the implementation.

What you will achieve: You will clean, analyze, chart, and summarize data by describing what you want in plain English, with AI writing and executing the code behind the scenes, reading files from your Drive, and producing downloadable results you can share immediately.

Note

How AI runs code on your data

Both Claude and ChatGPT have built-in code execution environments. When you upload a spreadsheet or CSV, the AI can write Python code to process it, run that code in a secure sandbox, and return the results in the form of cleaned data, charts, summary statistics, or even new spreadsheet files. Claude calls this feature **code execution** or **artifacts**. ChatGPT calls it **Advanced Data Analysis**. The capability is the same: your AI tool becomes a data analyst that takes instructions in English.

Which tool for which data task

Claude and ChatGPT overlap heavily on data work, but each has rough edges and strengths that matter once you move past simple operations. The following table is a practical guide for picking between them on the kinds of tasks this chapter covers. Treat it as a starting point rather than a rule — capabilities on both sides change quickly, and the gap between them narrows with every release. If you only have access to one, the workflows in the rest of the chapter still apply; you may just need to compensate with an extra prompt or a manual step here and there.

Task	Best tool	Why
Clean a messy CSV or spreadsheet	ChatGPT (Advanced Data Analysis)	The sandbox runs Python directly on uploaded files. Best for heavy data manipulation.
Summarize and explain data	Claude (code execution)	Stronger at producing narrative summaries and combining data analysis with written explanations.
Generate charts and visuals	Both produce charts	ChatGPT produces charts inline. Claude generates interactive visuals via artifacts.
Read a spreadsheet from Google Drive	Claude (Drive integration)	With Drive connected, Claude reads Google Sheets directly. No download or upload needed.

Task	Best tool	Why
Quick calculation or formula help	Either	Both handle formula generation and explanation well.

Table 8.1 – Use ChatGPT for heavy data wrangling, Claude for analysis with narrative, and either for charts and quick calculations

Two considerations sit alongside the choice of tool, and they apply regardless of which one you settle on. The first is what data you can responsibly put into either system, since spreadsheets tend to carry more sensitive information than emails or transcripts. The second is what to do when the full code execution capability is not available to you, whether because you are on a free tier, your organization has restricted it, or the relevant connector is not enabled. Both considerations come up often enough in practice that they are worth treating directly before we move on to the workflow.

Data privacy and sensitivity

Spreadsheets often contain sensitive information: revenue figures, employee data, customer details, financial projections. Before uploading data to any AI tool:

- **Check your organization's data policy.** Some organizations prohibit uploading internal financial data to external AI tools. If yours does, ask whether an enterprise AI deployment with data residency guarantees is available.
- **Anonymize where possible.** If you need to analyze patterns but not identify individuals, remove names, email addresses, and employee IDs before uploading. The analysis works the same on anonymized data.
- **Use the Drive integration rather than downloads.** Reading a Google Sheet via Claude's Drive integration keeps the data within the Google-to-Anthropic trust boundary rather than downloading it to your local machine and re-uploading it.

Fallback: When code execution is unavailable

If you are on a free tier without code execution, the AI can still help with data work; it just cannot run code directly. Do this instead:

- **Formula generation:** Input this prompt: `Write me an Excel formula that calculates year-over-year growth for each row.` Copy the formula into your spreadsheet.
- **Analysis instructions:** Input this prompt: `Tell me step by step how to create a pivot table in Google Sheets that shows revenue by region and quarter.`
- **Data description:** Paste a sample of your data and ask the AI to identify patterns, outliers, or issues. It cannot run code but can reason about the data.

The connected, code-execution version is dramatically faster, but the fallback still saves time compared to figuring out formulas and procedures yourself.

The data analysis workflow

Every data task in this chapter follows a three-step pattern: load, describe, review.

Step 1: Load your data

You have three ways to get data into the AI:

- **Upload a file:** Drag a CSV, Excel file (`.xlsx`), or even a PDF table into the conversation. Both Claude and ChatGPT accept file uploads.
- **Read from Google Drive:** With Drive connected to Claude, you can ask it to read a Google Sheet directly: `Read the spreadsheet called 'Q4 Sales Data' from my Drive.` This doesn't require downloads or uploads.
- **Paste directly:** For small datasets, copy from your spreadsheet and paste into the conversation. This works for anything under a few hundred rows.

> Tip
>
> **Always start with "describe the data"**
>
> Before asking for analysis, ask the AI to describe what it sees: `Read this file and tell me: how many rows and columns, what the columns are called, and flag any obvious issues like missing values, mixed data types, or duplicates.` This catches problems before they corrupt your analysis.

Step 2: Describe what you want

This is the core skill. You do not tell the AI what formula to write or what code to run. You describe the outcome you want. The AI figures out the implementation.

Here's what bad instructions (implementation-focused) look like:

- `Write a XLOOKUP to match column A with Sheet 2 column B`
- `Create a pivottable with regions as rows and quarters as columns`

Here's what good instructions (outcome-focused) look like:

- `Show me total revenue by region for each quarter`
- `Which salesperson had the highest growth rate compared to last year?`

When you describe the outcome, the AI chooses the best method. It might use a pivot table, a group by operation, a custom calculation, or a combination. You get the answer faster because you are not constraining the solution to a specific technique.

Step 3: Review and iterate

The AI produces its analysis and shows you the result. Review it the same way you would review a colleague's work:

- **Do the numbers make sense?** Sanity-check headline figures against your expectations. If total revenue is $50M and you know it should be around $45–55M, it is probably right. If it says $500M, something went wrong in the data.
- **Are the categories correct?** Did the AI group things the way you expected? Misgrouping (combining two regions, splitting one product into two) is a common error with messy data.
- **Is anything missing?** Were any rows dropped during cleaning? Are all time periods included?

If something is wrong, describe the problem in plain English:

```
The revenue totals look too low. I think rows with "pending" status were excluded.
Include all rows regardless of status and add a column showing status breakdown.
```

Iteration is where the conversational nature of the tool earns its keep. Instead of rewriting the analysis from scratch, you are pointing at what looks off and asking the AI to fix that specific thing, with the rest of the work preserved. Most real analyses go through two or three rounds of this before the output is ready to share.

Three worked examples

The following three scenarios cover the most common data tasks knowledge workers face: cleaning a messy export, summarizing survey responses, and reconciling two related spreadsheets. Each example follows the load-describe-review pattern and shows the kind of prompt that produces usable results on the first or second pass. The prompts are deliberately verbose. Being specific about format, output, and edge cases is what separates a useful analysis from one that needs three rounds of clarification.

Example 1: Sales data cleanup

You have a CSV export from your CRM with 2,000 rows of sales data. It is messy: inconsistent date formats, duplicate entries, missing values in the "region" column, and revenue stored as text with currency symbols. Input this prompt:

```
I have uploaded a sales data CSV. Please:

1. Describe the data: rows, columns, data types
2. Clean it:
   - Standardize all dates to YYYY-MM-DD format
   - Remove duplicate entries (same deal ID)
   - Fill missing region values using the salesperson's most common region
   - Convert revenue to numeric (strip currency symbols and commas)
3. Show me a summary: total revenue, count by region, count by status
4. Flag any rows that could not be cleaned and explain why

Give me the cleaned file as a downloadable CSV.
```

The AI writes Python code to perform each cleaning step, runs it, and produces a clean CSV you can download. It also shows you a summary of what was changed: how many duplicates were removed, how many dates were reformatted, and how many missing regions were filled. This audit trail lets you verify the cleaning was correct.

Example 2: Survey result summarization

You conducted an internal survey with 200 responses and need to present the results to leadership. The data has Likert scale responses (1–5), free-text comments, and demographic fields. Input this prompt:

```
I have uploaded survey results (200 responses). Please:

1. For each Likert-scale question, show: mean, median, and distribution (how many
```

```
1s, 2s, 3s, 4s, 5s)
2. Generate a bar chart for the 5 most important questions showing the
distribution
3. Analyze the free-text comments: identify the top 5 themes and give 2
representative quotes for each
4. Break down satisfaction scores by categories; are any categories significantly
lower than average?
5. Write a 200-word executive summary of the results suitable for a leadership
presentation

Save the charts as images I can use in a slide deck.
```

The AI processes the quantitative data (statistics, charts, breakdowns) and the qualitative data (theme extraction from free-text) in the same conversation. The output is a complete analysis package: charts, statistics, theme summary, and a written executive summary. What would take most users half a day is done in 15 minutes.

Example 3: Budget variance analysis

You have two spreadsheets: the approved budget and the actual spend to date. You need to identify where you are over or under budget and explain the variances. Here is the prompt:

```
I have two files:
- Budget: approved budget by department and category
- Actuals: actual spend to date, same structure

Please:
1. Match budget to actuals by department and category
2. Calculate variance (actual - budget) and variance percentage for each line
3. Flag anything over budget by more than 10%
4. Generate a chart showing the top 10 variances (largest overspend and
underspend)
5. Write a 150-word narrative explaining the key variances, suitable for a finance
review meeting

Give me the combined analysis as a downloadable Excel file with the chart
embedded.
```

The AI reads both files, matches them, calculates variances, generates a chart, writes the narrative, and produces a downloadable Excel file. You could hand this directly to your finance team or paste the narrative into a meeting brief after having validated it (*Chapter 4*).

Tip

Ask for the narrative, not just the numbers

The most underused capability in data analysis is asking the AI to explain what the numbers mean. `Write a 200-word summary of these results for someone who has not seen the data` produces an insight paragraph that saves you from staring at a spreadsheet trying to decide what the story is.

Integrating your Drive for a fully automated workflow

With Google Drive connected, the data workflow becomes fully automated. You do not download, upload, or export anything:

```
Read the Google Sheet called "Monthly Revenue Tracker" from my Drive. Then:

1. Summarize this month vs last month: total revenue, growth rate, top-performing
product
2. Generate a line chart showing revenue trend for the past 6 months
3. Write a 3-sentence summary for my weekly status report
4. If revenue declined in any product category, flag it and suggest what I should
investigate

Save the chart to my Reports folder in Drive.
```

The AI reads your live Google Sheet, analyzes it, generates the chart, writes the summary, and saves the output back to Drive. The entire cycle – from data to insight to deliverable – happens in one conversation without you opening a spreadsheet application.

This connects directly to the *Chapter 6* document generation chain. The summary and chart from this prompt can feed into a status report: `Now use this analysis as input and generate my weekly status report following my template in Drive.`

When to trust the numbers

AI data analysis runs real code on your real data, which means the calculations are usually correct. But *usually* is not *always*. Here is when to verify:

- **Always check the row count.** If you uploaded 2,000 rows and the analysis is based on 1,800, find out what happened to the other 200. The AI may have dropped rows during cleaning without telling you.
- **Sanity-check totals against a known figure.** If you know total revenue should be approximately $10M and the AI says $9.8M, that is plausible. If it says $93M, the AI misread a column or applied the wrong unit.
- **Watch for grouping errors.** "Revenue by region" requires that the AI correctly identifies which column is the region. If your data has both "sales region" and "billing region," the AI might pick the wrong one.
- **Be careful with percentages and rates.** Growth rate, conversion rate, and percentage change are where subtle errors hide. A growth rate calculated as (new – old) / old is different from (new – old) / new. If the number matters, ask the AI to show its formula.

> Tip
>
> **Ask to see the code**
>
> If a calculation matters enough to act on, ask the AI: `Show me the code you used to calculate the growth rate.` You do not need to understand Python to spot a formula error. The AI will explain what the code does in plain English alongside the code itself.

Summary

In this chapter, you learned to -

- **Work with datasets:** sales data cleanup, survey result summarization, and budget variance analysis – each producing a complete deliverable.
- **Read data from cloud storage:** AI reads Google Sheets from Drive, analyses them, and saves results back to Drive. No download/upload cycle.
- **Verify analysis outputs:** when to verify (row counts, totals, groupings, rates) and how to ask the AI to show its work.

The time shift: a data task that took 2–3 hours of formula-writing and formatting now takes 20–40 minutes of describing, reviewing, and iterating. The skill shift may matter even more: you no longer need to know how to build a pivot table or write an XLOOKUP. You need to know what question to ask about your data.

We will cover content creation in depth in the next chapter, where will learn how to produce professional communications across multiple formats by writing once and repurposing everywhere.

Get this book's PDF version and more

Scan the QR code (or go to `packtpub.com/unlock`). Search for this book by name, confirm the edition, and then follow the steps on the page.

UNLOCK NOW

Note: Keep your invoice handy. Purchases made directly from Packt don't require an invoice.

9

Write Once, Use Everywhere

You ship a new feature. Now you need a LinkedIn post, an internal Slack announcement, a client email update, three bullet points for the sales deck, and a paragraph for the monthly newsletter. The information is the same, but the format, tone, length, and audience are different every time. Manually writing six versions of the same news is a spectacular waste of your time.

Connected AI solves this with a single input and multiple outputs. You provide the core content once: the facts, the context, the key message, and the AI produces every format you need, adapted for each audience. With Gmail and Drive connected, it can distribute them too.

What you will achieve: You will turn a single set of inputs into LinkedIn posts, internal announcements, client updates, presentation outlines, and newsletter sections, with AI reading your source material from Drive and distributing the results via email.

Building your style bank

A **style bank** is a collection of your best content pieces that the AI uses as a reference for future writing. It solves the *"this does not sound like our brand"* problem.

Save your best examples to a dedicated folder in Google Drive:

- 3–5 LinkedIn posts that performed well
- 2–3 client emails that struck the right tone
- Your company's voice guidelines or brand document (if one exists)
- Internal announcements you were pleased with

Then reference the bank in your prompts:

```
Before generating, read my Style Bank folder in Google Drive. Match the tone and
style of those examples.
Specifically:
- LinkedIn: match the hook style from my top posts
- Client email: match the warmth level from my example client communications
- Internal: match the casual, celebratory tone
```

Over time, the style bank becomes your content DNA. New team members can produce on-brand content by referencing the same bank. The AI learns your patterns from examples rather than relying solely on abstract rules.

> Tip
>
> **Update the bank quarterly**
>
> Every three months, swap out weaker examples for stronger, more recent ones. Your content style evolves; the bank should evolve with it.

Five content templates

The following prompts cover the most common professional content needs. Each is designed for connected AI reading source material from Drive or Gmail. Please replace the square brackets with your own inputs.

Template 1: Thought leadership post

This prompt will help generate a LinkedIn post about a particular work product that you want to be public about:

```
I want to write a LinkedIn post about [topic]. Read [document/meeting packet] from
my Drive for context.

Structure: hook (first line that stops the scroll), 2-3 paragraphs of insight, a
closing question or takeaway. 150-250 words. Professional but personal.

This is my voice, not a corporate announcement. Read my Style Bank folder for tone
reference.
```

Template 2: Project update (multi-audience)

This sample prompt will allow you to push an update to multiple stakeholders:

```
I need to communicate a project update. Read the latest meeting packet for
[project] from Drive and check [Asana/Linear] for completed tasks this week.

Generate three versions:
1. For my team (Slack): casual, focused on what shipped
2. For stakeholders (email): professional, focused on progress against milestones
3. For leadership (3 bullets): extremely concise, focused on status and risks
```

Template 3: Event or launch announcement

This sample prompt will help generate a well-structured announcement:

```
We are [launching / hosting / announcing] [thing].
Source: [paste details or point to Drive document].

Generate:
1. External announcement (LinkedIn/blog): 200 words
2. Internal announcement (Slack/email): 100 words
3. Press-friendly summary: 150 words, third person, factual, quotable
4. Social media teaser: 50 words max, punchy
```

Template 4: Recurring newsletter section

This prompt will allow you to aggregate information and send out a newsletter. Feel free to edit the prompt to reflect the newsletter audience, which might be internal or external.

```
It is time for this month's newsletter section. Read all meeting packets from the
past month in my Drive and check [Asana/Linear] for major completed items.

Write a 200-300-word section covering:
- Key accomplishments this month
- What is coming next month
- One highlight or story worth telling

Tone: [match newsletter examples in Style Bank].
Save to my Newsletter Drafts folder in Drive.
```

Template 5: Response to feedback or press

This sample prompt will allow you to reply to press:

```
Read this [article / review / feedback] about us:[paste or point to source].

Draft three response options:
1. Grateful and brief (if positive)
2. Constructive and measured (if critical)
3. Factual correction (if inaccurate)

I will pick the appropriate one. Do not combine them.
```

The content repurposing chain

The chain follows a three-step pattern: source and generate, review, and distribute.

Step 1: Provide the source material

The source material can come from anywhere in your connected ecosystem:

- A meeting packet from Drive (product launch discussion)
- A document or research brief from Drive (feature spec, analysis)
- An email thread from Gmail (client conversation with the core update)
- Raw notes you type directly (bullet points, key messages)

Here's a prompt you can use (add your source material and replace the bracketed placeholders with your own inputs):

```
I have news to communicate across multiple channels.

Source material:
- Read the meeting packet from [Meeting name] meeting in my Drive
- Also read the feature spec document titled "[Feature Name] v2 Spec" from Drive

Key message: [one sentence summarizing the core news]
Tone guidance: [exciting / measured / informational]

Using the source material above, generate the following content pieces:

1. LINKEDIN POST (150-200 words): Professional but engaging. Include a hook in the
first line. End with a question or call to action.
```

```
2. INTERNAL ANNOUNCEMENT (100-150 words): For Slack or internal email. Casual,
celebratory. Include what shipped, why it matters, and who to thank.

3. CLIENT EMAIL UPDATE (200-250 words): Professional, warm. Focus on what this
means for the client. No internal jargon.

4. PRESENTATION BULLETS (5-7 bullets): For a slide in our monthly all-hands deck.
Each bullet one line. Lead with impact.

5. NEWSLETTER PARAGRAPH (80-100 words): For the monthly company newsletter. Third
person, factual, concise.

Adapt tone, length, and framing for each audience. The facts must be identical
across all five.
```

With this one prompt, you get five outputs. The AI reads the source material once and produces all five pieces, each calibrated for its audience. The facts stay consistent because they all draw from the same source. The framing, tone, and length vary because the audiences differ.

Step 2: Review and edit

Five outputs in one pass means five places where something might be slightly off, and the goal of this step is to catch and fix the genuinely important ones rather than rewrite everything. Read the pieces in order of stakes, not in the order the AI produced them. The client email and the LinkedIn post are public-facing and carry the highest reputational cost if they go out wrong, so they get the first and most careful pass. The internal announcement and the presentation bullets matter less if a phrase is awkward. The newsletter paragraph usually needs the least attention because the format is so constrained.

What you are looking for is narrower than line editing. Three things are worth checking on every piece:

- Are the facts the same across all five? If the LinkedIn post says the feature shipped to all customers and the client email says it shipped to enterprise customers first, one of them is wrong. Cross-check numbers, dates, names, and any specific claims.

- Does the tone actually fit the audience? The AI tends to drift toward a generic upbeat register on announcements. Read each piece imagining the actual reader: would your most skeptical client respond well to this email, or would the enthusiasm read as overselling? Would the internal Slack post sound natural from you, or would your team find it stiff?
- Is there anything you would not say in your own voice? Phrases that feel a little too polished, claims you cannot personally stand behind, jargon you would not use in a meeting. Strike them.

Then loop back with targeted edits rather than starting over:

```
The client email is mostly good, but the second paragraph oversells. Tone it down
so it reads as informational rather than promotional. Also, the LinkedIn post hook
is too generic, try one that opens with the specific customer problem we solved.
```

Two or three rounds of this are normal. The AI keeps everything else stable while it adjusts the specific things you flagged, so you are not re-reviewing pieces that were already fine. Stop iterating when the pieces sound like things you would have written yourself with more time, not when they are perfect.

Step 3: Distribute

With email connected, you can distribute directly from the conversation:

```
The content looks good. Please:
- Send the client email update to [client contacts] via Gmail with subject:
"[Subject]"
- Send the internal announcement to [team email] via Gmail
- Save the LinkedIn post and newsletter paragraph to my Content folder in Google
Drive
- I will paste the presentation bullets into the deck manually
```

Two emails sent, two pieces saved to Drive, and one pasted manually. The entire cycle from source material to distributed content can save you a lot of time, letting you focus on verification and quality control.

When to write from scratch

AI-assisted content works brilliantly for informational, promotional, and operational communication. It works less well when the content IS the work:

- **Personal essays and reflections:** If your audience values your perspective specifically, writing is thinking. AI can help you organize thoughts, but the thinking should be yours.
- **Sensitive communications:** Layoff announcements, crisis responses, apologies. The stakes are too high for any miscalibration in tone.
- **Content that builds relationships**: A handwritten note to a mentor, a personal recommendation letter. The effort is part of the message.

The rule: if the recipient would care whether you wrote it yourself, write it yourself. For everything else, let AI handle the first draft and focus your energy on making it right.

Summary

In this chapter, you have learned how to -

- **Generate content across platforms:** One set of source material produces LinkedIn posts, internal announcements, client emails, presentation bullets, and newsletter paragraphs
- **Push to cloud storage:** Emails drafted via Gmail – ready to be sent, documents saved to Drive, all from one conversation
- **Create a tone reference:** Your best content examples that the AI references for tone and brand consistency

Content creation is where every workflow in this book converges. Meeting packets become announcements. Research briefs become thought leadership. Task completions become status updates. Data analysis becomes newsletter highlights. The connected AI system you have built across *Chapters 3–8* is now a content engine.

The next and final chapter puts it all together: your complete automated week, from Monday morning brief to Friday status report.

Get this book's PDF version and more

Scan the QR code (or go to `packtpub.com/unlock`). Search for this book by name, confirm the edition, and then follow the steps on the page.

UNLOCK NOW

Note: Keep your invoice handy. Purchases made directly from Packt don't require an invoice.

10

Your Automated Week

Throughout this book, you have learned workflows for email, meetings, research, documents, tasks, data, and content. Each workflow has prompts you could copy and run manually. But the real power, the thing that makes this a system rather than a collection of tricks, is turning these workflows into reusable Skills that trigger automatically.

What you will achieve: You will install the companion Skills that make every workflow in this book automatic, connect your tools, and run the complete Monday-to-Friday system so that starting next week, AI handles the scaffolding and you do the thinking.

Technical requirements

A few practical notes before you start installing anything:

- **The examples in this chapter use Claude.** The screenshots, menu paths, and exact wording all come from Claude's interface, which is the tool we have leaned on most through the book. The Skills themselves are not Claude-specific, however; the same ZIP files in the companion repository install into ChatGPT and Perplexity as well, with slightly different upload steps that the repository documents in full. If you have been working through the earlier chapters on ChatGPT or Perplexity, you can follow the workflow in this chapter and substitute the installation steps from the repository for your tool of choice.
- **Both free and paid tiers work.** Every workflow in this book and every Skill in the repository can be run on a free tier, manual mode included. Paid tiers are not a gate; they are a friction reduction. A paid plan typically raises message limits, allows larger file uploads, and unlocks the connectors (Gmail, Drive, your task tool) that turn manual paste-in steps into automatic reads. Most people who use the full Monday-to-Friday system daily find one paid subscription pays for itself in time saved, but you do

not need one to install the Skills or follow this chapter. Start on whatever tier you are on and upgrade when the friction starts to bother you.

- **Your organization's policies still apply.** As discussed in earlier chapters, some organizations restrict which AI tools can access internal data. If you cannot connect Gmail or Drive for compliance reasons, every Skill in the repository is designed to fall back to manual mode: you paste content into the conversation instead of the AI reading it directly, and the rest of the workflow runs the same way. You lose the seamlessness of the connected version, but the time savings on the actual analysis and drafting work are preserved.

Every Skill from every chapter in this book is available as a ready-to-install package at: `https://github.com/PacktPublishing/AI-For-Everyday-Automation`

What is a Skill, exactly?

A **Skill** is a small bundle of instructions you give to your AI tool once, which it then follows whenever the situation calls for it. Mechanically, it is a folder containing a short text file (written in plain English, not code) that tells the AI three things: what the Skill is for, when to use it, and how to carry it out step by step. The folder can also include supporting files, such as templates, checklists, or example outputs, that the Skill draws on while it runs. The Skills in the companion repository are distributed as ZIP files, which are simply that folder compressed for upload.

Once installed, a Skill behaves like a colleague who has been briefed on a standard way of doing a particular task. When you mention that task in conversation, the AI recognizes it, pulls in the relevant Skill, and runs through the steps you defined, without you having to paste a long prompt or remember the right wording. You say, "check my email," and the *Inbox Zero Skill* runs. You say, "good morning," and the *Automated Week Skill* launches your full daily briefing. You ask for "the weekly status report," and the chain from *Chapter 6* fires automatically.

A useful way to think about it: the prompts you have been writing throughout this book are like notes you scribble each time you want to do something. A Skill is the same instruction, written down once in a place the AI always checks. Skills do not give the AI new capabilities it did not have before; they give it muscle memory for the specific workflows you care about.

A short demonstration

To make this concrete, the screenshot sequence on the following pages walks through installing and running the audit and automate Skill from the companion repository. You will see: the ZIP file being uploaded to Claude's Skills interface. The Skill itself is roughly twenty lines of plain-English instructions.

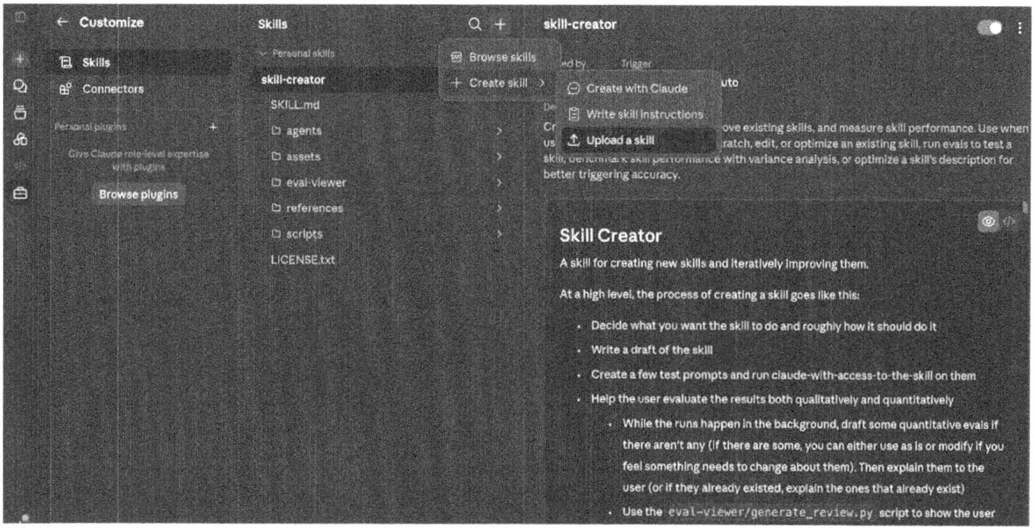

Figure 10.1 - Claude customize panel to upload the Skill zip

The following figure shows the confirmation that Claude has registered the Skill:

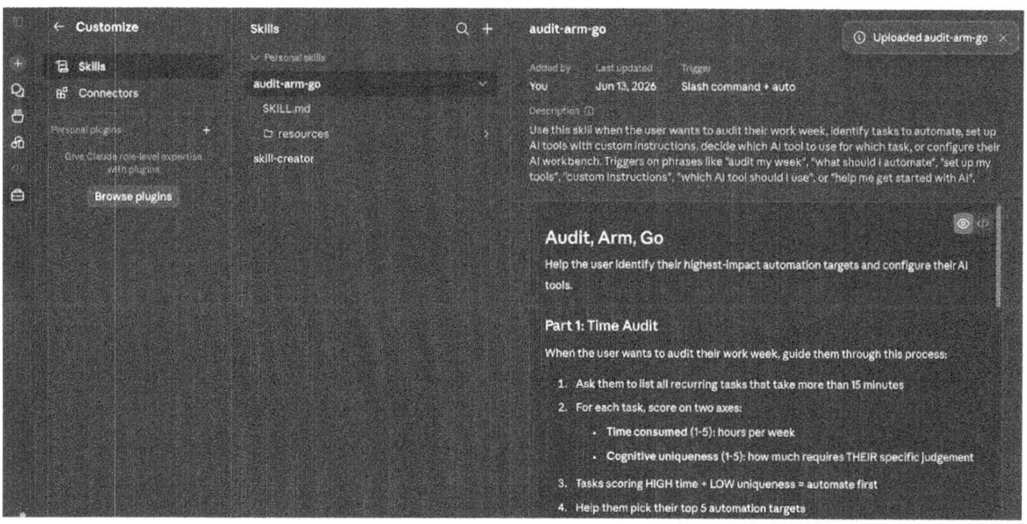

Figure 10.2 - The audit Skill registered on the interface

The next figure shows the Skill being triggered and Claude asking us for more information to help us with the automation.

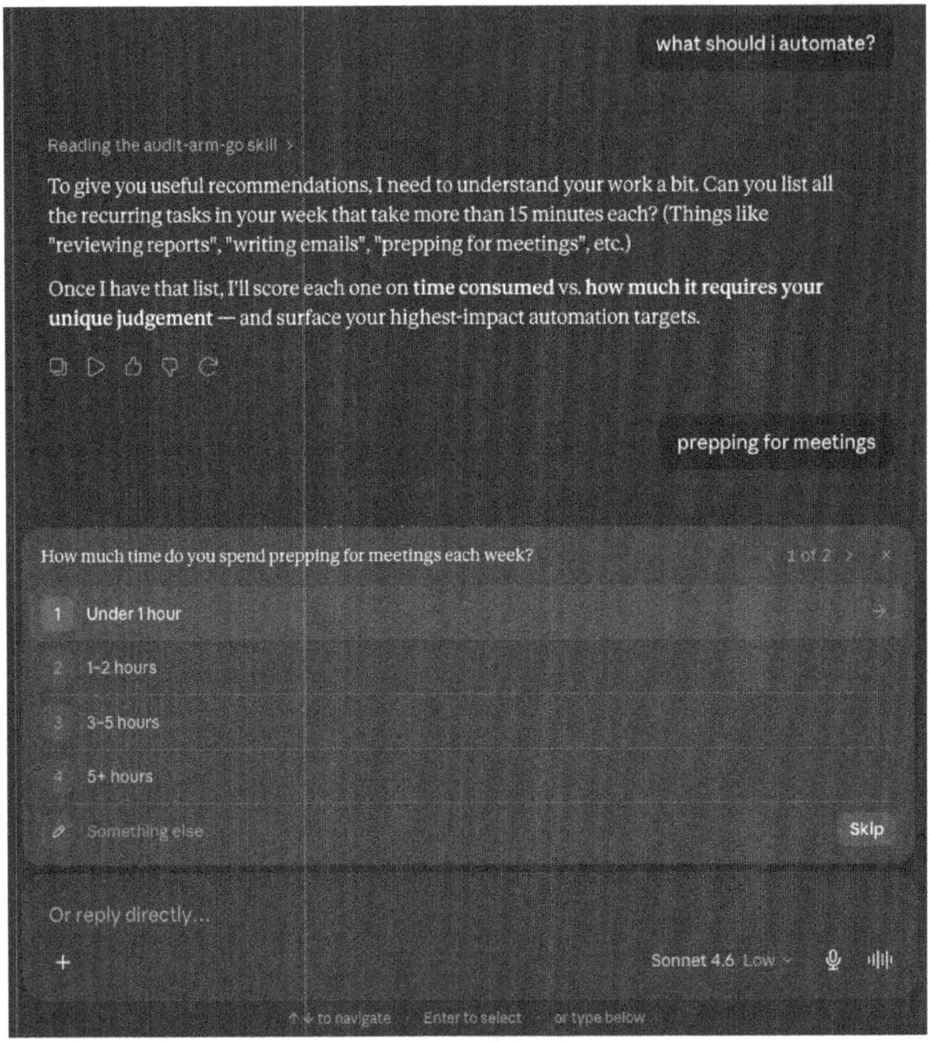

Figure 10.3 - Automation audit Skill

You do not need to read or edit the Skill file to use it. But it is worth opening one once, just to see how short and plain-spoken these files are. There is no magic to them, which is part of the point: once you have used the ones in this book for a while, writing your own for tasks specific to your work becomes a natural next step.

Installing the Skills

The installation process is a one-time setup that takes about 15 to 20 minutes the first time you do it, and most of that is waiting for files to download and Claude to acknowledge each Skill. The steps below walk through the full sequence: pulling the Skill files from the companion repository, uploading them into Claude, verifying each one is registered, and connecting the tools (Gmail, Drive, and your task tracker) that the Skills will eventually call. Work through these in order, since the later Skills assume the earlier ones are in place and the connector setup needs to be finished before any Skill that touches your data can run.

If you hit a step that does not match what you see on screen, the most likely cause is an interface change since this book went to print. Claude's settings layout shifts every few months. However, the principle of each step stays the same even when the exact menu name does not, so look for the equivalent option rather than the precise label.

Step 1: Download the Skill files

1. Visit `https://github.com/PacktPublishing/AI-For-Everyday-Automation`
2. Navigate to the `dist` folder. You will see a ZIP file for each Skill, plus an `all-Skills.zip` containing every Skill.
3. Download the Skills you want. If you are not sure where to start, download `01-audit-arm-go.zip`, `03-inbox-zero.zip`, and `10-automated-week.zip`; these cover setup, email, and the daily system.

Step 2: Upload to your AI tool

In Claude (recommended)

1. Go to `https://claude.ai/` and sign in
2. Click **Customize** in the left sidebar, then click **Skills**
3. Click the + button, then select **Upload a Skill**
4. Select the ZIP file you downloaded. The Skill will appear in your list.
5. Make sure the toggle next to the Skill is switched on
6. Repeat for each Skill you want to install

In ChatGPT

1. Go to `https://chatgpt.com/` and sign in
2. Click your profile icon, then select **Skills**

3. Click **New Skill**, then **Upload from your computer**
4. Select the ZIP file. The Skill is now active.

In Perplexity

1. Go to `https://www.perplexity.ai/` and sign in
2. Navigate to **Computer Skills**
3. Upload the ZIP file

> Note
>
> **You only install each Skill once**
>
> After uploading, the Skill stays in your account permanently. You can toggle Skills on or off at any time. If an updated version is released in the repository, download the new ZIP and upload it again to replace the previous version.

Step 3: Connect your work tools

The Skills work best when your AI tool can read your email, calendar, and documents directly. You set up each connection once and it persists across all conversations and Skills.

You do not need to connect everything at once, and trying to do so in a single sitting tends to slow you down because each integration requires its own OAuth approval and, depending on your organization, possibly a brief wait for IT to whitelist the connection. A more practical approach is to set the integrations up over the course of a few days, in the order shown in *Table 10.1*. This is also why the table is structured by day rather than by Skill: you connect the tool, give yourself a day to confirm it works on a low-stakes Skill, then move on to the next one. By the end of the week, the full system is in place.

If your organization has restricted some of these integrations, do what you can with the rest. The Skills are designed to fall back gracefully: a Skill that will normally read from Drive can still work if you paste the relevant content into the conversation, and one that would normally draft via Gmail can produce a draft for you to copy and paste. You lose some of the seamlessness, but the workflow itself still saves time.

Day	Connect	How (in Claude)	Skills unlocked
1	Gmail	**Customize → Integrations → Gmail → Authorize with your Google account**	03 Inbox Zero

Da y	Connect	How (in Claude)	Skills unlocked
2	Google Calendar	**Customize → Integrations → Google Calendar → Authorize**	04 Meetings
3	Google Drive	**Customize → Integrations → Google Drive → Authorize**	05 Research, 06 Docs, 08 Data
4	Task tool	**Customize → Integrations →** search for `Asana/Linear/Notion` **→ Authorize**	04 Meetings, 07 Tasks

Table 10.1 - Integration setup schedule. Each connection takes about 5 minutes. You only do this once

Tip

Start with Gmail only

If connecting four services feels like too much, connect Gmail on Day 1 and stop there. The email Skill alone saves 45–60 minutes a day. Add Calendar on Day 2 when you see the value. Build gradually.

Detailed setup instructions for each tool and integration are in the *Appendix*.

Which Skills to install first

You do not need all ten Skills to start. Pick based on where you spend the most time:

If you spend too much time on...	Install this Skill	Say this to trigger it
Figuring out where to start	01-audit-arm-go	`Help me figure out what to automate`
Your first AI task	02-first-ai-win	`Help me try AI on a real task`
Email	03-inbox-zero	`Check my email`
Meeting prep and follow-up	04-meetings	`What meetings do I have today?`

If you spend too much time on...	Install this Skill	Say this to trigger it
Research	05-research	`Research the market for [X]`
Drafting reports and documents	06-first-drafts	`Write my weekly status report`
Tracking tasks and action items	07-task-extraction	`What did I commit to this week?`
Spreadsheets and data	08-data-analysis	`Analyze this spreadsheet`
Content and communications	09-content-on-demand	`Write a LinkedIn post about this`
All of the above	10-automated-week	`Good morning (Monday), Good morning. Run my weekly close (Friday)`

Table 10.2 - Skill selection guide. Start with one or two. Add more as you build confidence

The system in action

With the Skills installed and your tools connected, here is what a typical week looks like. You no longer need detailed prompts. You talk naturally and the Skill handles the rest.

Monday morning

Open Claude (or your preferred tool) and input this prompt:

```
Good morning. It is Monday.
```

The *Automated Week Skill* activates and does everything at once: checks your calendar for the full week, reads your task tool for overdue and upcoming items, triages your Gmail inbox with draft replies, generates pre-meeting briefs for today's meetings, and suggests your top priorities. You review for 15–20 minutes and your Monday is organized.

Daily rhythm (Tuesday–Friday)

The following table shows how the Skills can be used to organize your everyday work:

Time	What you say	What the Skill does
8:30 AM	`Good morning`	Skill 10: today's meetings with briefs, email triage with drafts, task priorities, overdue items.
9:00	`[review + approve]`	Skill 03: you review the email drafts, provide intent for specific replies, and click send.
After meetings	`Here is the transcript`	Skill 04 + 07: generates packet, emails attendees, creates tasks in your tracker, saves to Drive.
As needed	`Research [X] / Draft a report`	Skill 05 / 06 / 08: research, documents, or data analysis reading from Drive and connected tools.
3:00 PM	`"Check my email"`	Skill 03: second email session. Same triage-draft-approve cycle.
5:00 PM	`Anything I missed today?`	Skill 07: checks today's emails and transcripts for untracked commitments.

Table 10.3 - The daily rhythm. Skills fire automatically at each touchpoint. Deep work fills the space between

Friday close

Use this prompt:

```
It is Friday. Run my weekly close.
```

This is the same `Skill 10` you used on Monday, now responding to a Friday trigger. It runs the full close-out sequence: it reconciles your task portfolio across your task tool, Drive, and Gmail; generates your weekly status report and emails it to your manager; previews next week's calendar and flags meetings needing prep; and optionally drafts a LinkedIn post or internal update about the week's highlights. One sentence from you can produce four deliverables.

Week one checklist

Here is exactly what to do in your first five days. Each day adds new Skills and new integrations.

Day	What to do	Skills to install	Time
Mon	Complete the *Chapter 1* audit. Set up custom instructions. Connect Gmail. Install Skills and run the email workflow.	01, 02, 03	30 min
Tue	Connect Google Calendar. Install meeting Skill. Get your first morning brief. Process your first meeting transcript.	04	20 min
Wed	Connect Google Drive and your task tool. Install research and task Skills. Try a research task. Extract tasks from a meeting.	05, 07	25 min
Thu	Install document and data Skills. Run a document generation chain on a real report. Try data analysis if you have a spreadsheet.	06, 08	25 min
Fri	Install the weekly system and content Skills. Run the Friday close. Measure your time savings. Update your voice guide.	09, 10	20 min

Table 10.4 - Week One schedule. By Friday, all 10 Skills are installed, and the complete system is running

By Friday evening, you have: ten Skills installed, four integrations connected, and a week's worth of experience with the system. Many readers can save 8–12 hours in their first full week.

Measuring your time savings

Track the first two weeks to prove the value to yourself. A simple table works:

Task	Before (estimated)	With Skills (actual)	Time saved (Estimated)
Email (2 sessions/day)	90 min/day	45 min/day	45 min/day
Meeting overhead (6/day)	3 hrs/day	1 hr/day	2 hrs/day
Research (2/week)	5 hrs/week	1.5 hrs/week	3.5 hrs/week
Status report (weekly)	90 min	20 min	70 min
Task coordination (daily)	45 min/day	15 min/day	30 min/day
Estimated weekly total			8–12 hours

Table 10.5 - Sample table helping you track AI-driven time savings

After two weeks, stop tracking. The workflows are habits and the savings are self-evident. If you are not saving at least 5 hours a week after two weeks, revisit your *Chapter 1* audit; you may be automating the wrong tasks.

> Tip
>
> **Track quality too**
>
> Time saved is the obvious metric. Also notice: are your emails more consistent? Are meeting follow-ups happening faster? Are tasks falling through the cracks less often? Is your status report better structured? Quality improvement is often worth more than the time savings.

Keeping your Skills current

AI tools evolve fast. The Skills in this book are designed around durable patterns, but specific capabilities change. Here is how to stay current:

- **Check the repository for updates.** Visit `https://github.com/PacktPublishing/AI-For-Everyday-Automation` periodically. Updated Skills will be published there as AI tools add new features or change their interfaces.
- **Update a Skill by re-uploading.** Download the new ZIP, go to your **Skills** panel, and upload it. The previous version is replaced automatically.
- **Customize for your needs.** Each Skill is a plain text file you can edit. If a workflow does not match your job perfectly, open the SKILL.md, adjust the instructions, re-zip the folder, and upload the customized version. The Appendix explains how.

Sharing Skills with your team

If you are on a Claude Team or Enterprise plan, you can share Skills with your entire organization:

1. Install the Skill in your own account first
2. In the **Skills** panel, click on the Skill you want to share
3. Click **Share** and choose whether to share with specific people or your entire organization
4. Recipients see the Skill in their Skills list and can toggle it on

This is the fastest way to standardize workflows across a team. New hires install the shared Skills and are productive on day one.

> Note
>
> **Team-wide consistency**
>
> When everyone on a team uses the same meeting Skill, every meeting produces an identical packet format. When everyone uses the same status report Skill, reports are consistent and comparable. When everyone uses the same task extraction Skill, nothing falls through the cracks. Shared Skills are not just a convenience; they are an organizational operating system.

Where to go next

Through the workflows in this book, you've hopefully managed to set up a system that lets you save time at work every week. But we've barely scratched the surface, and the possibilities for what you can do with AI are endless. Let's discuss a few ways in which you can continue your learning beyond this book.

Build your own Skills

As you develop custom workflows specific to your role, build them as Skills. A Skill is just a `SKILL.md` file in a folder, zipped, and uploaded. The *Appendix* walks through creating a custom Skill from scratch.

Watch for AI agents

The Skills in this book are the first step toward autonomous AI agent systems that monitor your calendar, email, and task tools continuously and act without being prompted. As agent capabilities mature, the manual "say good morning" step will become a background process. The Skills you have installed define the tasks, data sources, and approval gates that agents will automate end to end.

Stay connected

The repository at `https://github.com/PacktPublishing/AI-For-Everyday-Automation` is the living companion to this book. New Skills, updated workflows, and community contributions are published there as the landscape evolves.

The one thing that matters

This book promised one outcome: reclaim a full working day every week. The Skills you have just installed are the mechanism. They encode every workflow, prompt chain, and connected automation from the preceding nine chapters into packages that fire automatically when you need them.

The tools will change and the Skills will be updated, but the underlying pattern will not: describe what you need, let connected AI handle the mechanical work, review the output, and focus your irreplaceable human judgment on the decisions that actually matter. That is the AI-powered workday.

Get this book's PDF version and more

Scan the QR code (or go to `packtpub.com/unlock`). Search for this book by name, confirm the edition, and then follow the steps on the page.

UNLOCK NOW

Note: Keep your invoice handy. Purchases made directly from Packt don't require an invoice.

11

Unlock Your Exclusive Benefits

Your copy of this book includes the following exclusive benefits:

Follow the guide below to unlock them. The process takes only a few minutes and needs to be completed once.

Unlock this Book's Free Benefits in 3 Easy Steps

Step 1

Keep your purchase invoice ready for *Step 3*. If you have a physical copy, scan it using your phone and save it as a PDF, JPG, or PNG.

For more help on finding your invoice, visit `https://www.packtpub.com/en-us/unlock?step=1`.

> Note
>
> **Note**: If you bought this book directly from Packt, no invoice is required. After *Step 2*, you can access your exclusive content right away.

Step 2

Scan the QR code or go to `packtpub.com/unlock`.

On the page that opens (similar to *Figure 11.1* on desktop), search for this book by name and select the correct edition.

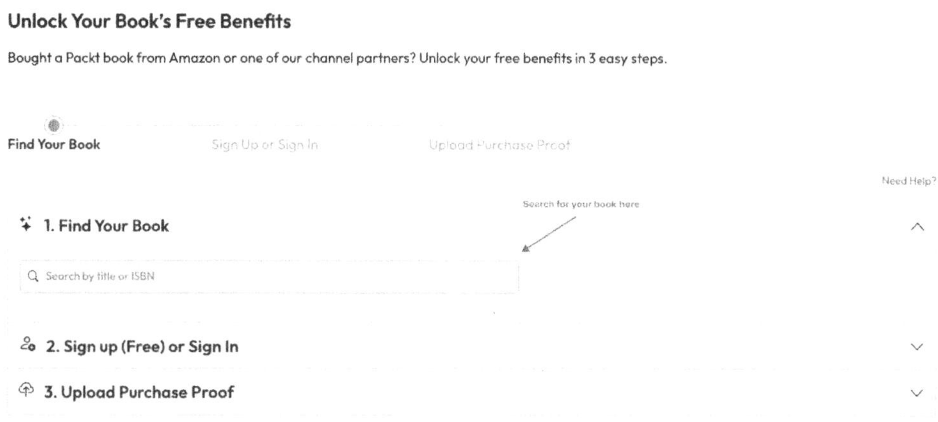

Figure 11.1: Packt unlock landing page on desktop

Step 3

After selecting your book, sign in to your Packt account or create one for free. Then upload your invoice (PDF, PNG, or JPG, up to 10 MB). Follow the on-screen instructions to finish the process.

Need Help

If you get stuck and need help, visit `https://www.packtpub.com/unlock-benefits/help` for a detailed FAQ on how to find your invoices and more. This QR code will take you to the help page.

> Note
>
> **Note**: If you are still facing issues, reach out to `customercare@packt.com`.

Appendix

Setup and Skill Installation Guide

This appendix covers everything you need to get up and running: creating accounts, installing Skills, connecting integrations, setting up your Google Drive, and customizing Skills for your specific needs. Use it as a reference: find the section you need, follow the steps, return to the chapter.

We'll cover the following topics:

- Downloading the companion Skills
- Installing Skills in Claude
- Installing Skills in ChatGPT
- Installing Skills in Perplexity
- Claude Account setup and custom instructions
- ChatGPT Account setup
- Connecting integrations in Claude
- Meeting transcription setup
- Setting up your Google Drive folders
- Customizing Skills for your needs
- Troubleshooting
- Companion resources

> **Note**
>
> **Interfaces change frequently**
>
> AI tool interfaces update regularly. The steps below describe the intent of each action rather than exact button locations. If something has moved, visit the Skills repository for updated instructions with current screenshots: `https://github.com/PacktPublishing/AI-For-Everyday-Automation`

A.1 Downloading the companion Skills

1. Visit `https://github.com/PacktPublishing/AI-For-Everyday-Automation` in your web browser
2. Click the green **Code** button, then **Download ZIP** to get everything at once. Or navigate to the `dist` folder and download individual Skill ZIPs.
3. Unzip the download if you downloaded the full repository. Inside you will find a `dist` folder containing one ZIP per Skill, ready to upload.

The individual Skill ZIPs in `dist` are the files you upload to your AI tool. Do not unzip them; upload the ZIP file directly.

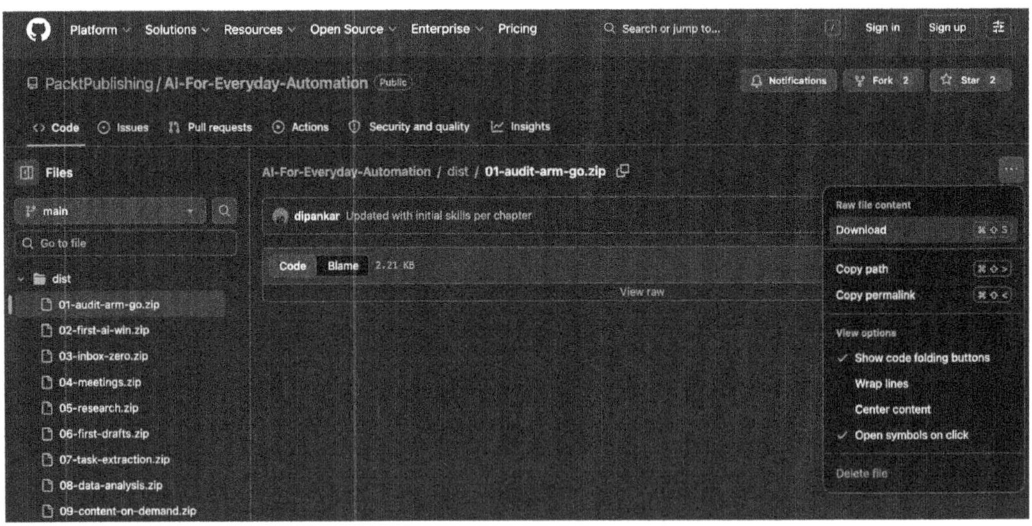

Figure A.1 - Downloading the Skill ZIP file from GitHub

A.2 Installing Skills in Claude

At the time of writing, Claude supports custom Skills on Free, Pro, Max, Team, and Enterprise plans. Code execution must be enabled.

Enabling Skills

1. Go to `https://claude.ai` and sign in
2. Navigate to **Settings** (gear icon) → **Capabilities**
3. Ensure **Code execution and file creation** is toggled on
4. Navigate to **Customize** (in the left sidebar) → **Skills**. This is your Skills management panel.

Uploading a Skill

1. In the **Skills** panel, click the + button
2. Select **Upload a Skill**
3. Choose the ZIP file (e.g., 03-inbox-zero.zip) from your downloads
4. The Skill appears in your list. Make sure the toggle next to it is switched on.
5. Repeat for each Skill you want to install

Verifying a Skill works

After installing, open a new conversation and try the trigger phrase listed in the *Chapter 10* Skill map. For example, after installing `03-inbox-zero`, say `check my email`. If the Skill activates and begins reading your Gmail, it is working. If it does not, check that the Skill toggle is on and that code execution is enabled.

Updating a Skill

Download the new version of the ZIP from the repository. Upload it again using the same process. The previous version is replaced.

Removing a Skill

1. Find the Skill in your **Skills** panel
2. Toggle it off to disable (keeps it in your list) or click the **...** menu and select **Delete** to remove it entirely

A.3 Installing Skills in ChatGPT

ChatGPT supports Skills on Business, Enterprise, Edu, and Healthcare plans. The feature may also be available on Plus plans; check your account settings.

1. Go to `https://chatgpt.com/` and sign in
2. Click your profile icon, then select **Skills**
3. Click **New Skill**, then **Upload** from your computer
4. Select the `ZIP` file from your downloads
5. The Skill is now active and will trigger automatically in conversations

The same Skills work in both Claude and ChatGPT. The `SKILL.md` format is understood by both platforms. If a Skill uses an integration (like Gmail) that is not available in ChatGPT, the Skill will still work but will ask you to provide the information manually.

A.4 Installing Skills in Perplexity

1. Go to `https://www.perplexity.ai/` and sign in
2. Navigate to **Computer Skills** in your settings
3. Upload the `ZIP` file

Perplexity Skills are most useful for the research Skill (`05-research`), which takes advantage of Perplexity's built-in sourced search. Other Skills that depend on Gmail or Calendar integrations are better used in Claude or ChatGPT.

A.5 Claude account setup and custom instructions

Claude is the AI tool most of the workflows in this book lean on, particularly the ones in later chapters that depend on Skills, Drive integration, and the connector ecosystem. The following steps cover the minimum setup you need to follow the chapters end-to-end: creating an account, choosing a tier that matches how you plan to use the system, and configuring custom instructions so Claude knows enough about your role and preferences to be useful from the first conversation. None of this takes more than ten minutes, and the custom instructions in particular are worth a few minutes of thinking, since they apply to every conversation you have from that point on.

Creating an account

1. Visit `https://claude.ai` and sign up with your email or Google account
2. Verify your email address
3. The free tier provides access to Claude. You can do most activities in the book with the free tier at the time of publication. Pro adds higher limits, file uploads, and Projects.

Custom instructions

1. Open **Settings** (gear icon or profile menu)
2. Find the **Custom Instructions** or **Profile** section
3. Paste your custom instruction text from the template in *Chapter 1* (also available as `resources/custom-instructions-template.txt` inside the `01-audit-arm-go` Skill)
4. Save. Your instructions now apply to every new conversation and every Skill.

Claude Projects (optional)

If you prefer to organize workflows into dedicated workspaces rather than using Skills, Claude Projects offer an alternative. Create a Project, paste a SKILL.md's contents into the Project Instructions, and upload reference documents. Each conversation in the project inherits those instructions. However, Skills are recommended over Projects because Skills trigger automatically across all conversations, while Projects require you to open the specific project.

A.6 ChatGPT account setup

1. Visit `https://chatgpt.com/` and sign up
2. At the time of writing, the free tier provides access to GPT-4o. Plus adds higher limits and Advanced Data Analysis.

Custom instructions

1. Click your profile icon → **Settings** → **Personalization** → **Custom Instructions**
2. Fill in both fields using the template from *Chapter 1*
3. Save. These apply to all conversations.

Advanced Data Analysis

Advanced Data Analysis lets ChatGPT run code on uploaded files. It is available on Plus and higher plans. Upload a CSV or Excel file in any conversation and ChatGPT will write and execute Python code automatically. This powers the data analysis Skill (08-data-analysis).

A.7 Perplexity account setup

1. Visit `https://www.perplexity.ai/` and create an account
2. Free tier provides standard search with citations. Pro adds deeper analysis, file uploads, and higher limits.
3. In Settings, explore Focus modes for narrowing search to specific source types (Academic, News, etc.)

A.8 Connecting integrations in Claude

Claude connects to external services through its integrations panel. Each connection is authorized once and persists across all conversations and Skills.

Google Calendar

1. In Claude, go to **Customize** → **Integrations** (or look for the connector icon near the input box)
2. Select **Google Calendar**
3. You will be redirected to Google's authorization page. Sign in and grant access.
4. Return to Claude. Test: `What meetings do I have today?`

Google Drive

1. Same path: **Customize** → **Integrations** → **Google Drive** → **Authorize**
2. Test: `Search my Drive for [a document you know exists]`

Gmail

1. **Customize** → **Integrations** → **Gmail** → **Authorize**
2. This allows read access for your emails Test: `Read my latest unread email and summarize` it

Task tools (Asana, Linear, Notion, Jira)

1. **Customize** → **Integrations** → search for your tool
2. If available, select and authorize
3. Test with this prompt: `Show me my` `open tasks`

If your tool is not listed, check the repository for workarounds and newly added connectors.

Note

Enterprise and Workspace accounts

If you use a work account managed by your organization (Google Workspace, Microsoft 365), some integrations may require admin approval. If the authorization step fails or shows an "admin admins to provision organization-wide integrations.

A.9 Meeting transcription setup

The meetings Skill works from a transcript, which means the system is only as good as whatever is recording your meetings in the first place. Most readers will already have a transcription tool in place through their organization, since Zoom, Google Meet, and Teams now all ship with built-in transcription that often produces a usable output without any third-party setup. If you do not have one, or if the built-in version your organization uses produces transcripts you cannot easily export, a dedicated tool fills the gap.

The following setup covers Otter.ai, which is the most widely used standalone option and the one the Skills in the companion repository have been tested against. Equivalent tools (Fireflies, Fathom, Read.ai, tl;dv) work the same way at a high level: connect a calendar, let the tool join calls automatically, and export transcripts when you need them. If you are already on one of those, skip to the export step at the bottom and confirm the output format is plain text the AI can read.

Otter.ai

1. Visit `https://otter.ai/`and create an account
2. Connect your calendar (Google Calendar or Outlook) so Otter can see your meetings
3. Enable auto-join for video calls. Otter will join Zoom, Google Meet, or Teams meetings automatically.
4. Configure speaker identification: add team members' names so Otter labels speakers correctly
5. After meetings, export the transcript as text for use with the meetings Skill

Fireflies.ai

1. Visit `https://fireflies.ai/`and create an account
2. Connect your calendar and enable auto-join
3. Configure integrations (Slack, Notion, Asana) for automatic summary distribution

Built-in transcription

Zoom (AI Companion), Google Meet, and Microsoft Teams all offer built-in transcription. Enable it in your platform's settings. Transcripts are available in the meeting recording section after the call. The meetings Skill works identically regardless of transcription source.

A.10 Setting up your Google Drive folders

Several Skills save outputs to Google Drive. Create these folders once so Skills can find them by name:

- `Meeting Packets`: structured meeting summaries from the meetings Skill (*Chapter 4*)
- `Research`: research briefs from the research Skill (*Chapter 5*)
- `Status Reports`: weekly status reports from the documents Skill (*Chapter 6*)
- `Content`: LinkedIn posts, announcements, newsletter drafts from the content Skill (*Chapter 9*)
- `Templates`: your document outlines and prompt chain templates (*Chapter 6*)
- `Style Bank`: your best content examples for AI style reference (*Chapter 9*)

Create these in your Google Drive. The Skills reference them by name when the meetings Skill says, `save to my Meeting Packets folder`, the AI searches your Drive for a folder with that name.

A.11 Customizing Skills for your needs

Every Skill is a plain text file inside a ZIP. You can edit them to match your specific workflows.

How to edit a Skill

1. Unzip the Skill file on your computer. Inside, you will find a folder with a `SKILL.md` and optionally a `resources/` subfolder.
2. Open `SKILL.md` in any text editor (Notepad, TextEdit, VS Code—anything works)
3. Edit the instructions. Common changes: adjusting trigger phrases in the description field, changing tool names (e.g., replacing "Asana" with "Jira"), adding company-specific language, or modifying output formats
4. Save the file
5. Re-zip the folder (select the folder, right-click, click **Compress/Zip**)
6. Upload the new ZIP to your AI tool, replacing the previous version

What to customize

- **Trigger phrases:** The description field at the top of `SKILL.md` controls when the Skill fires. Add phrases your team uses naturally ("stand-up notes" instead of "meeting packet," "weekly sync" instead of "status report").
- **Tool names:** Replace [Asana/Linear/Notion] with your specific tool.
- Output formats: If your organization has a specific meeting packet format or status report template, edit the Skill to match.
- **Resource files:** Add your own templates, style guides, or reference documents to the resources/ folder. The Skill can reference them.

Building a Skill from scratch

A Skill is any folder containing a `SKILL.md` file with a `YAML` frontmatter block:

```
---
name: My Custom Workflow
description: Use this Skill when the user asks to
  [describe the trigger conditions in natural language].
---

# My Custom Workflow

[Write the instructions the AI should follow. Be specific about steps, output
format, and which integrations to use.]
```

Save this as `SKILL.md` inside a folder named after your Skill. Zip the folder. Upload.

> Tip
>
> **Start by editing, not building**
>
> Before creating a Skill from scratch, try editing an existing one. Take the closest Skill to what you need, modify the instructions, and re-upload. Most custom workflows are variations of the ten Skills in this book.

A.12 Troubleshooting

Skill is installed but does not activate

- Verify the Skill toggle is on in your **Skills** panel

- Check that Code execution and file creation is enabled in **Settings → Capabilities**
- Try being more explicit: `Use my inbox zero Skill` to check my email
- Check that the SKILL.md's description field contains phrases matching your request

Integration shows connected, but AI cannot read data

- Try disconnecting and reconnecting the integration (**Customize → Integrations →** click the service → disconnect, then reconnect).
- Verify that you authorized the correct Google account (work vs. personal).
- For Google Workspace accounts, check that your organization's admin has not restricted third-party access.

Gmail send failure

- Verify that send permission was granted during authorization (not just read access)
- Reconnect the Gmail integration and ensure you click **Allow** on the send permission screen

Drive search returns nothing

- Drive search matches on document titles, not content. Use specific, descriptive folder and file names.
- Ensure the document is in your Drive (not in Shared Drives that may have different permissions).

Skill upload fails

- Ensure the ZIP contains a single folder with a SKILL.md file inside it
- Check for invalid characters in the folder name (use only letters, numbers, and hyphens)
- Verify the file is a proper ZIP, not a renamed folder

Skills grayed out (Team/Enterprise)

An organization admin must enable both Code execution and Skills in **Organization Settings → Skills**. Contact your admin.

A.13 Companion resources

The Skills repository at `https://github.com/PacktPublishing/AI-For-Everyday-Automation` is the living companion to this book. It contains:

- All ten Skills as ready-to-upload ZIPs

- Resource files (custom instructions template, voice guide template, Drive folder structure)
- Updated Skills as AI tools evolve
- A build script for regenerating ZIPs after customization
- A detailed README with visual diagrams showing how Skills connect

The book gives you the durable patterns and the thinking behind each workflow. The repository keeps the specific implementations current.

Other Books You May Enjoy

If you enjoyed this book, you may be interested in these other books by Packt:

Workflow Automation with Microsoft Power Automate

Aaron Guilmette

ISBN: 978-1-83664-963-2

- Build cloud flows using triggers, connectors, and actions
- Use Copilot and generative AI to create and edit flows
- Automate desktop tasks with Power Automate for Desktop
- Create approval processes for Teams, Slack, and email
- Connect Power Automate to Dataverse, Forms, and SQL
- Implement error handling, monitoring, and troubleshooting
- Govern and scale automations using best practices

Practical Generative AI with ChatGPT

Valentina Alto

ISBN: 978-1-83664-785-0

- Explore the fundamentals of generative AI and GPT models
- Master prompt engineering to consistently get relevant and reliable outputs from ChatGPT
- Develop marketing strategies and conduct meaningful A/B testing with AI assistance
- Boost your coding with code generation, review, and optimization
- Enhance research with real-time knowledge mining
- Enhance your visual creativity with image generation, image understanding, and style transfer
- Design custom GPTs and assistants tailored to specific business functions
- Discover how enterprises are leveraging large language models for their AI apps

The Power Platform Playbook for Digital Transformation

Victor Dantas, Chris Huntingford

ISBN: 978-1-80512-139-8

- Design and deploy end-to-end business solutions using Power Platform's low-code capabilities
- Automate processes and eliminate inefficiencies with low-code/no-code automation
- Implement Power Platform governance, security, and compliance best practices for enterprise success
- Integrate Power Platform with Microsoft 365, Dynamics 365, and third-party applications
- Develop a strategy for digital transformation and change management with real-world use cases
- Leverage AI-powered tools to optimize business workflows and enhance user experience

Packt is searching for authors like you

If you're interested in becoming an author for Packt, please visit `authors.packt.com` and apply today. We have worked with thousands of developers and tech professionals, just like you, to help them share their insight with the global tech community. You can make a general application, apply for a specific hot topic that we are recruiting an author for, or submit your own idea.

Share your thoughts

Now you've finished *AI for Everyday Automation*, we'd love to hear your thoughts! Scan the QR code below to go straight to the Amazon review page for this book and share your feedback or leave a review on the site that you purchased it from.

`https://packt.link/r/1808089812`

Your review is important to us and the tech community and will help us make sure we're delivering excellent quality content.

Index

P

R

S

T

V

W

Made in the USA
Monee, IL
16 September 2026

63035036R00090